THE STRANGER

D1610625

This book explores the concept of the stranger as a 'modern' social form, identifying the differing conceptions of strangerhood presented in the literature since the publication of Georg Simmel's influential essay 'The Stranger', questioning the assumptions around what it means to be regarded as 'strange', and identifying the consequences of being labelled a stranger.

Organised both chronologically and thematically, the book begins with Simmel's major essays on the stranger and culminates with an analysis of Zygmunt Bauman's thought on the subject, with each chapter introducing an idea or key theme initially discussed by Simmel before exploring the development of the theme in the work of others, including Schütz, Derrida, and Levinas. The stranger is an enduring concept across many disciplines and is central to contemporary debates about refugees, asylum, the nature of inclusion and exclusion, and the struggle for recognition. As such, this book will be of interest to scholars across the social sciences.

Shaun Best is a senior lecturer in the School of Education and Liberal Arts at the University of Winchester, UK. His teaching is in the field of social inclusion and exclusion, and he publishes regularly in national and intern: publications

including   **KA 0443046 8**   *ccessful Social*

Research ar

KEY IDEAS

Designed to complement the successful *Key Sociologists*, this series covers the main concepts, issues, debates, and controversies in sociology and the social sciences. The series aims to provide authoritative essays on central topics of social science, such as community, power, work, sexuality, inequality, benefits and ideology, class, family, etc. Books adopt a strong 'individual' line, as critical essays rather than literature surveys, offering lively and original treatments of their subject matter. The books will be useful to students and teachers of sociology, political science, economics, psychology, philosophy, and geography.

SERIES EDITOR: PETER HAMILTON

For a full list of titles in this series, please visit www.routledge.com/Key-Ideas/book-series/SE0058

THE STRANGER

Shaun Best

Routledge
Taylor & Francis Group

LONDON AND NEW YORK

First published 2019
by Routledge
2 Park Square, Milton Park, Abingdon, Oxon OX14 4RN

and by Routledge
52 Vanderbilt Avenue, New York, NY 10017

Routledge is an imprint of the Taylor & Francis Group, an informa business

© 2019 Shaun Best

British Library Cataloguing in Publication Data
A catalogue record for this book is available from the British
Library

Library of Congress Cataloging-in-Publication Data
A catalog record has been requested for this book

ISBN: 978-1-138-31219-7 (hbk)
ISBN: 978-1-138-31220-3 (pbk)
ISBN: 978-0-429-45837-8 (ebk)

Typeset in Bembo
by Taylor & Francis Books

MIX
Paper from
responsible sources
FSC
www.fsc.org
FSC™ C013985

Printed in the United Kingdom
by Henry Ling Limited

CONTENTS

INTRODUCTION

The practice of estrangement

> Social life is essentially practical. All mysteries which mislead theory to mysticism find their rational solution in human practice and in the comprehension of this practice.
>
> *(Marx 1959: 285)*

Human agents interact with one another; however, some of us are inter-acted with as strangers and others as 'normal' and 'familiar' people. This book deals with one of the most pressing issues of human life today; the inability of people to live with others. Most current military conflicts, terri-torial disputes and sectarian violence are related to people's inability to live together. *Strangers* are excluded from various aspects of social life in that they face barriers to participation that people who are not regarded as strangers do not face. Unusually although the stranger is 'not like us' they are not com-pletely unfamiliar or unknown to us, but different. The presence of the stranger can generate feelings of insecurity. The stranger may make us think about and question the taken-for-granted assumptions we make about our world. To question what it means to be normal, to think about the nature of limits and boundaries in all aspects of social life, including the physical, racial, aesthetic, sexual, national, legal and moral.

In 1937 Talcott Parsons published *The Structure of Social Action: A Study in Social Theory with Special Reference to a Group of Recent European Writers* (Parsons 1937). In 1998 the International Sociological Association claimed that the book was the ninth most important sociological book of the twentieth century. In this influential book Parsons outlined key points from the work of Alfred Marshall, Vilfredo Pareto, Emile Durkheim and Max Weber. In his review of the book for the *American Sociological Review*, Louis Wirth explained that: 'the book goes beyond the scope of a mere commentary by treating each writer in the light of all of the others'. Wirth found Parsons' approach: 'highly interesting and helpful in the diagnosis of our present-day battle of theories' (Wirth 1939: 400).

In this current book I have made use of the approach used by Parsons in 1937. The book is organised thematically around the work of five principal authors: Georg Simmel, Erving Goffman, Pierre Bourdieu, Norbert Elias and Zygmunt Bauman and attempts to go beyond a commentary of each single author to identify and evaluate the mechanisms of social inclusion and exclusion with reference to the sociological literature on the stranger. The argument in the book explores a practice-oriented conception of how individuals come to perceive the Other as a stranger. The central argument developed is that our fear of strangers involves a fear of strangeness and that the mechanisms that bring about a sense of community are the same mechanisms that generate estrangement. Estrangement is presented here as a categorisation process focused on the maintenance of in-group and out-group preconceptions that are internalised into our own consciousness as a set of negative and unkind attitudes towards the Other as a stranger. Oppression or discrimination against the stranger is then an actively co-created, constructed social relationship, based upon a set of practices propagated and maintained by people within the community. In addressing questions such as: 'What is the stranger? What is it that generates the sameness of us?' and 'Why does the stranger take such a rich variety of forms across the social sciences?', the book attempts to identify and explore the socio-political mechanisms of subjectification and related concepts such as habitualisation (Berger and Luckmann 1967) and the practical consciousness (Giddens 1979) that allow us to generate the category of the stranger.

In the Enlightenment modernist tradition, it is assumed that human beings should be treated as autonomous and rational people who should be included and treated with equal respect. Our individual idiosyncrasies are regarded as irrelevant to the equal respect which all people should be entitled to. As such any embodied difference between people should be regarded as irrelevant to the way people should be treated. Human beings understand each other through a common language and, in this respect, we feel we have something in common. Although for most of the time leading a life involves just getting on with the ordinary and routine aspects of everyday life, even the most mundane of our social actions are conducted inter-personally and we are all active participants (or practitioners) in our social worlds. How events and people make sense to someone and what is significant to us depend on our reading of practices that the person participates in, although many people would find it difficult to differentiate the action from the underpinning guidance contained within the practices that sustain it. When people participate in the same practices, they share intelligibility. As Simmel was to explore in his work, the recognition of ways of behaving and symbolism associated with it are the essence of sociality. By engaging in social actions, we strengthen the social cohesion of the social structure that we share. When it comes to the processes of estrangement, people make sense to a given person by attempting to read their behaviour in relation to their own practice. If we cannot understand what the Other is doing or saying, the Other will lack intelligibility for us. The stranger may attempt to participate in unfamiliar practices to develop an understanding of them perhaps to become included, but they remain a stranger.

Hypothetically human agency allows the individual to behave however they like whenever they like. Despite this, most of us, most of the time, choose not to act without reference to the feelings and opinions of others. Practice is the guidance that we draw upon in any situation when deciding the appropriate way to behave. In other words, practices are ways of behaving with reference to cognitive and symbolic structures of knowledge that make possible the agent's ability to interpret 'shared knowledge' that facilitates a shared way of ascribing meaning to the world. Practices then guide us on the ways of performing activities in everyday life, from the ways of cooking our dinner, the ways of consuming it, the ways of working, to the ways of crossing the road.

This is not to suggest that human behaviour is determined or totally predictable. There are many ways of making an omelette or a fruit salad, just like there are many was of taking a free kick in a football match. Although individual human agents can be viewed as the carriers of a practice, there are many ways of behaving that draw upon the same conception of practices. As such practices shape but do not determine the ways in which we behave in any given circumstance, but they do guide and shape our perception. As human agents we must choose the appropriate way of behaving and interpret how to apply the practice in the given circumstance. Choosing to conform is still a choice.

Individuals live within a 'community of practice' that Wittgenstein has described as a 'form of human life'. According to Baker and Hacker, for Wittgenstein:

> A form of life is a way of living, a pattern of activities, actions, interactions and feelings which are inextricably interwoven with, and partly constituted by, uses of language. It rests upon very general pervasive facts of nature. It includes shared natural and linguistic responses, broad agreement in definitions and judgements, and corresponding behaviour.
>
> *(Baker and Hacker 2009: 74)*

People who live within a community share common practices, in that they are guided in similar situation to draw upon similar resources that guide us on how to behave. In this way the community encourages its members to become homogeneous agents by eliminating individual unconventional behaviours, such as disgusting habits composed of intolerable oddness, bizarreness and strangeness. We 'read' the people with whom we are co-present and judge if they are complete members of the community of practice and share our form of life. Within a community of practice people share the same language, discourse and traditions that help to generate an underpinned by common conception of reasonableness. As Lingis suggests:

> The rational elaboration of significant symbols transforms our biological specificity, making our species one composed of individuals representative of a universal community. ... The man-made species

we are, which produces its own nature in an environment it produces, finds nothing within itself that is alien to itself, opaque and
impervious to its own understanding.

(Lingis 1994: 9)

As members of a *community of practice* we come to understand each other
because we share the same language and the same system of symbols. We
behave and act in response to each other in what is read as the appropriate
and predictable way. However, there are some people who do not share
language with us, and who do not behave and act in response to each other
in what is read as the appropriate and predictable way. Such people can find
themselves placed outside of the community of practice and labelled as
strangers and/or foreigners. In addition, people who undergo a life transformation can find themselves placed outside of the practice community
and find themselves undergoing a form of Othering and become strangers:
displacement, poverty, mental health issues, and disability are amongst some
of the many factors that can lead to precariousness (Bourdieu, Butler,
Lorey), liminality (Goffman, Turner) or estrangement.

In this book social exclusion leading to estrangement is identified as
having three overlapping levels of abstraction. First, intra-personal exclusion or a personal feeling of being potentially an outsider or stranger; when
an individual has a personal understanding that they are not fully a
member of the community in that they believe they have a distinctive,
individual feature that makes them unrepresentative of the others within
the community. If possible, such individuals may attempt to hide the feature that makes them feel different, or alternatively to actively campaign
for the difference to be regarded as insufficient grounds for exclusion.
Second, inter-personal exclusion when an individual chooses to act within
a face-to-face encounter in such a manner as to exclude the Other and
identifying the Other as a stranger. Third, structural exclusion, where the
barriers to participation in social life appear to be external to the individual,
such as exclusion on the grounds of class, race, gender or sexuality.

What is practice?

Theories of human agency commonly assume that people's activities
start with intentionality; a subjective meaning, motive or intention that

is prior to our behaviour. Practice theory often assumes that much human behaviour is habitual and takes place without such detailed reflection. Practice-based theories are commonly associated with the work of Pierre Bourdieu and Anthony Giddens. Bourdieu's work will be addressed in a later chapter.

The concept of the knowledgeable agent is the central concept in Giddens' structuration theory. Giddens' theory of structuration views society as being recursively created through the practices of individual human agents. Ways of behaving that we feel comfortable with can be applied in similar situations repeated over and over again. For Giddens a central concept in understanding everyday practice is the practical consciousness. Practical consciousness is a concept derived from Harold Garfinkel to describe a non-discursive, but not unconscious, knowledge of social institutions – as involved in social reproduction (Giddens 1979: 24): 'practical consciousness: tacit knowledge that is skilfully applied in the enactment of conduct, but which the actor is not able to formulate discursively' (Giddens, 1979: 57). The practical consciousness is our pattern recognition ability: the ability to make a judgement if an observed behaviour stands in a relation to a previously observed pattern of action. Pattern recognition is then the ability to compare a series of currently occurring actions with a known set of previous actions that we successfully interpreted.

Discursive consciousness describes a capacity for awareness and or knowledgeability about social conditions and the opportunities for action that human agents feel are appropriate in the given circumstance: 'The giving of reasons in day-to-day activity, which is closely associated with the moral accountability of action, is inevitably caught up in, and expressive of, the demands and the conflicts entailed within social encounters' (Giddens 1979: 58).

Even though our knowledge of the situation may be difficult to articulate, our feelings of uncomfortableness or awkwardness in situations are a product of our reflection on practices. We feel at our most uncomfortable when we are unaware of the most appropriate way to behave in a situation we find ourselves in or when the behaviours we have witnessed appear to be inappropriate. Practices help to make human action predictable within a given time and place. The practical consciousness is used by Giddens to explain that the actions of the human agent are not determined by forces outside of the individual. Giddens argues that human agents can establish rules and routines for themselves. The practical consciousness is one of three concepts that Giddens uses to define human agency; the other elements are the unconscious and the discursive consciousness. The unconscious is a concept derived from Freud to outline those elements of our self which we are not fully in control of and which are beyond our immediate intentions, while the discursive consciousness is a term derived from Alfred Schütz to suggest that individuals have the ability to reflect upon their social actions to make sense of these actions. Schatzki (2002) develops Giddens' conception of practical consciousness to suggest that people are capable at identifying contexts and situations and then choosing what they consider to be the appropriate way of behaving within the situation.

Practice is drawn upon by individuals to provide meaning to social life and guide action. The principal authors who are addressed in each of the chapters, Simmel, Goffman, Bauman, Elias and Bourdieu, are concerned in the last analysis with an understanding of the stranger that is based upon a chain of reason or set of justifications that is nothing more than defining a person as strange based on a set of psychological dispositions shared within a community.

Although he explains that practices are beyond habit, have a relatively plastic quality and vary in terms of their complexity and dimensions, Michael Oakeshott defines a practice as follows:

> A practice may be identified as a set of considerations, manners, uses, observances, customs, standards, canon's maxims, principles, rules, and offices specifying useful procedures or denoting obligations or duties which relate to human actions and utterances. It is a prudential or a moral adverbial qualification of choices and performances, more or less complicated, in which conduct is understood in terms of a procedure.
>
> *(Oakeshott 1975: 55)*

Similar ideas are also taken up by Charles Taylor (1985), who suggests that practice is a set of concerns 'out there' that directs how people choose to act. Practices are not a set of individual actions. Rather practice is a 'mode of relations' or 'mutual actions' that may have a rule-like quality, but it does not stipulate specific ways of behaving; however practice does allow the person some understanding of the possible consequences of choosing to behave one way rather than another. Practice identifies the acceptability of ways of behaving. Stephen Turner (1994) explains how people come to acquire their understanding of practices:

> the only access we have to [practices] is through our own 'culture.' From the point of view of what we can know about them, or how we can construct them, they are irredeemably cultural facts. We need a starting point within culture to recognize something else as practice .... So the very constitution of a practice as an object is tainted by our starting point, which is itself a contingent fact which we can neither understand nor overcome.
>
> *(Turner 1994: 103)*

Schatzki (1997: 110) argues that there can be no meaning without understanding and practices are a 'central constitutive phenomenon in social life' because it is with reference to practice that understanding is arranged and intelligibility communicated.

The starting point for Simmel's understanding of the stranger, for example, was just such a form of normative structuration. From a Kantian perspective, Kantians' experience alone cannot produce human cognition. The mind, which can go beyond experience, imposes on universal and necessary categories of reason. However, Kantian a priori categories assume social stability; for Simmel when the conditions providing stability are lifted, for example under conditions of rapid social change as Simmel himself experienced in late nineteenth-century and early twentieth-century Berlin, the individual must move beyond the limits of intelligibility that Kant identified. In a pragmatist style, Simmel holds on to or rather attempted to hold on to what he viewed as valuable in the empiricist and the Kantian positions. As such our perception of the world is driven by a need to view people and objects in terms of categories. Human reason works with categories, but these categories are not intrinsic or inborn in humans but are produced in the activities of people. Our experience of the world is always mediated, we perceive the world through categories that we have acquired though our socialisation into the culture of the society we live. As such the world is always a social world and our categories are always social categories. However, because the categories of thought are never a perfect reflection of experience, we must develop the capacity to think for ourselves and to appreciate the perspectives of others.

Our criteria for intelligibility are no longer adequate because the world around us has changed. There are no longer the same fixed boundaries around what is thinkable and intelligible; nonetheless, thought must start from somewhere and that somewhere is the already familiar. When we come across a person who does not behave in a way that conforms to what Wittgenstein calls 'our techniques', or our structured ways of doing things, we are unable to fully understand what they do as meaningful. For Wittgenstein we may even feel that we are in the presence of mad people:

> The madness would be like this: (a) The people would do something which we'd call talking or writing. (b) There would be a close analogy between our talking and theirs, etc. (c) Then we would suddenly see an entire discrepancy between what we do and what they do – in such a way that the whole point of what they are doing seems to be lost, so that we would say, 'What the hell's the point of doing this?'
>
> *(Wittgenstein 1989: 203)*

The principal authors explored in this book approach the issue of the stranger from their own distinct vantage points and each draws upon a different perspective in sociology. However, each of them shares something similar to Wittgenstein's contextualist view of intelligibility and the context provided by a practice. Wittgenstein scholar Stanley Cavell argues that Wittgenstein is concerned with identifying the: 'philosophical practice of the ordinary' (Cavell 1988: 264); Cavell explains that for Wittgenstein practice: 'constitutes ... a way or weave of life' (Cavell 1988: 263). Practice contains guidance that people will heed to if only 'doubtfully'. Our assessments of intelligibility are then necessarily context-dependent. It is for this reason that Simmel's analysis of social forms or forms of life, moves beyond a Kantian interpretation. As has already been suggested, social change means that in the urban environment we come across behaviours and situations that are not wholly recognised by the a priori categories that previously supported practices. The a priori categories can no longer give epistemic support to understanding behaviours that are now unintelligible or beyond the limits of the what was previously intelligible. When new circumstances present themselves and the previous categories are no longer fit for purpose, we can move beyond the old boundaries for thought or redefine the boundaries; in Wittgenstein's terms we are 'always building new roads for traffic; by extending the network of the old ones' (Wittgenstein 1978: 166).

Practices are prescriptions about how things ought to be done, they are a resource that we draw upon to enable us to think and then act meaningfully. Practices provide the epistemic foundations for social action. Drawing on Heidegger's phenomenological notion of 'being-in-the-world' and Wittgenstein's concept of 'intelligibility', Theodore Schatzki (1996) describes how practices provide meaning for physical actions and forms of communication, including the use body language in a manner that makes action meaningful for self and others. The actions of individuals are understood as meaningful because they are linked and interconnected. We have a practical understanding of an action because underpinning the action we observe is a normative order that we are familiar with. The actions and our descriptions of action (including the way we describe actions to ourselves) that come to form a practice:

> constitute a nexus [that] is to say that they are linked in certain ways. Three major avenues of linkage are involved: 1) through understandings, for example, of what to say and do; 2) through explicit rules, principles, precepts and instructions; and 3) through what I will call 'teleoaffective' structures embracing ends, projects, tasks, purposes, beliefs, emotions and moods.
>
> *(Schatzki 2002: 201)*

To make something intelligible is to make that something understandable; intelligibility is concerned with providing meaningfulness and choosing the appropriate emotional response. Intelligibility is then a feature of personal explanation building in respect to actions we observe and communications we receive. For something to be intelligible it must be captured by the intellect. Although intelligibility is concerned with the criteria the individual draws upon to make something understandable, intelligibility and understanding and are not identical. Most often we draw upon intelligibility criteria habitually, but occasionally we come across something that we are uncertain about and we must search for a best fit form within the forms that we are already familiar with. We search for resemblance to recognise, describe and understand. As suggested above, social change disrupts our understanding of the world and as such our criteria for intelligibility must change over time. Human agents can revise the criteria or categories they use to makes sense of the content of an action and provide form to something that they are coming across for the first time.

When we come across a stranger there are certainties that we have because we recognise that the person before us is a 'person'. There are certain needs and ways of acting shared by all human beings. So, we understand that this individual will need water to survive, breathe air and that this person will have language to communicate but we may not understand it; these are certainties and are part of the form that we draw upon to understand more about the person before us. However, beyond these basic certainties, the stranger is a person who is initially unintelligible to us. The stranger is not like us, the stranger may have socio-cultural differences, in that they appear to violate some conditions of meaningfulness for us. As Gertrude Conway suggests: 'One could say that all humans participate in the human form of life, but that there can be different forms of human life' (Conway 1989: 78).

Within a community there is a form of life that participants/practitioners regard as right and that they choose to live their lives by. Wittgenstein discusses this in relation to the idea of bedrock within his conceptions of 'form of life' and 'certainty'. In *On Certainty*, Wittgenstein looks at certainty as an attitude that underpins practice: 'some things that one does not doubt' (Wittgenstein 1972: 337). However, participants/practitioners also understand that there are different forms of human life. There is an indirect sense of dependence with a community that we rarely think about because it is followed habitually. As Wittgenstein (1989) suggests, this indirect sense of dependence is a necessary pre-condition for practice; participants/practitioners agree on what they do, in that by and large they all do the same thing, in that their actions display a degree of uniformity. When it comes to people we are unfamiliar with, their behaviours are different from our own, and we may ask ourselves: What type of person acts like that? When coming into contact with the stranger intelligibility is often concerned with the imposition of a categorical identity. It is not uncommon to find in racist discourse that the stranger is denied the status of a human form of life and described as a nonhuman form of life; by for example the use of an animal metaphor, such as swarms of migrants. To describe someone as leading a nonhuman form of life, is to define that person as less than human and provides the basis for a categorical exclusion of the stranger. If the categorically excluded person is crying out in pain, we may not regard their distress as the same experience as the distress that people who are fully human experience.

In summary, practices are customary or regular ways of understanding, or non-subjective forms of understanding and knowing that underpin our everyday performances. We interpret our performances in relation to other people's behaviour and interpretation. Practices make our behaviours understandable to observers who share the same culture. Andreas Reckwitz (2002) explains that practice is: 'a routinized type of behaviour which consists of several elements, interconnected to one other: forms of bodily activities, forms of mental activities, "things" and their use, a background knowledge in the form of understanding, know-how, states of emotion and motivational knowledge' (Reckwitz 2002: 249).

Practice can be habitual, but it also has both creative and agentic elements in terms of facilitating the freedom to act or in informing the subjective experience of agency; as identified in a range of very different theories including Giddens' theory of structuration, Bourdieu's notion of habitus, Schatzki (1997) on practice, Garfinkel (1967) on membership, and others.

During our involvement in the social world we constantly create and re-create our understanding of the social world. When presenting ourselves in everyday life we adopt a reflexive attitude towards self and Other. We may only notice this reflexive aspect of self when we fail to read or fully understand the behaviour or actions of the Other, or the normal flow of social action is disrupted for some reason. If a person can identify a tomato as a fruit, we may praise their knowledge of fruit and vegetables but if they put a tomato in a fruit salad we would question their taste or knowledge of cookery. Such forms of disruption may make us question the values, attitudes and beliefs or symbols in Simmel's phrase, that we and other people use in our attempts at meaning-making, perhaps leading to a more abstract interpretation of the events that unfold before us.

The presence of the Other can often provide an opportunity to reflect on the way in we choose to lead our lives and in informing how we should treat the Other in future contacts. In addition, practice is understood as an activity that people do in everyday life. The outcome of which provides the constituting underpinning for social order and a resource for the processes of Othering and estrangement. As such, practice, identity, social action, Othering and estrangement are linked. The argument developed here is that estrangements are living practices and in each of the chapters the principal author acts as a guide or narrator who is concerned with one or more specific aspects of estrangement.

By searching for the mechanisms of estrangement in terms of practice, the barriers to participation that strangers face are understood to be found in the 'situated activities' of individual human agents: the mundane activities that make up everyday life. Social exclusion is then a product of the thoughts and feelings of individual people that guides their actions and decisions to treat others as different, generating barriers to participation and creating a category of person that is known in the literature as 'the stranger'.

In Berger and Luckmann's terms it is possible to rethink the process of habitualisation; to rethink the natural attitude in relation to people and behaviours that are currently categorised as strange. When we do something for the first time it can be a great challenge. However, the more often we do that thing the less challenging it becomes. Berger and Luckmann suggest that behaviours that we repeatedly carry out come to be 'habitualised'. As individuals we get used to competing social actions in a way that has worked for us in the past and allows us to achieve our desired objective:

> Habitualisation carries with it the important psychological gain that choices are narrowed. While in theory there may be a hundred

ways to go about the project of building a canoe out of match-sticks, habitualisation narrows these down to one. This frees the individual from the burden of 'all those decisions', providing a psychological relief.

(Berger and Luckmann 1967: 71)

From within the context of our own culture, habitualisation allow people to steadily develop an understanding of appropriate patterns of behaviour and appropriate forms of communication for both self and Other, although our understanding is never complete as new ways of behaving and new contexts emerge. In most situation we have a clear understanding of the expectations of how to behave and what is appropriate to say in the given circumstances: what Berger and Luckmann describe as 'the natural attitude'.

It is this conception of habitualisation that underpins Berger and Luckmann's (1967) conception of social construction. Social life is underpinned by a duality; an 'objective' and a 'subjective' reality. It is through the process of habitualisation that our subjective meanings come to have an objective feel that is external to self:

It will be enough, for our purposes, to define 'reality' as a quality appertaining to phenomena that we recognize as having a being independent of our volition (we cannot 'wish them away'), and to define 'knowledge' as the certainty that phenomena are real and that they possess specific characteristics.

(Berger and Luckmann 1967: 13)

Individuals always have a subjective understanding of reality, but at the same time the individual internalises the natural attitude but retains the ability to contribute to the natural attitude if they feel it is appropriate. Individuals make sense of the social world by relating what they experience to their own subjective familiarities, and then choose to act based on that subjective interpretation. When we come to recognise patterns of behaviour, we come to treat that pattern as 'typical'. If our interpretation is confirmed by the behaviour of others, then Berger and Luckmann describe this as a typification; people reciprocally typify each other's actions. Typification is the basis for common behaviours as when two individuals come to typify each other's actions, this allows the formation of a stable relationship. Social construction is then based upon the assumption that the individual is in a dialectic relationship with society, that individuals are competent and can create and recognise rules and routines, as such individuals possess agency.

In her review of the nature and role of habit, Wendy Wood (2017) argues that 'habit mechanisms' sustain self-regulation. It is commonly assumed that when people repeat actions in the same context, the influence of habit increases and the influence of intention decreases. Individuals may impart intentionality onto their habits, mistakenly regarding externally prompted thoughts and understandings as their own choices (Loersch and Payne 2011). According to Campbell (1963: 97), in a similar fashion to attitudes, goals, personality traits and stereotypes, habits reflect 'residues of experience of such a nature as to guide, bias, or otherwise influence later behavior'. Wood (2017) also explains that William James (1890: 3) believed: 'habit covers a very large part of life' and assumed that habits have an abstract quality and act as a symbolic, conservative force in society. Neal, Wood and Drolet (2013) argue that in circumstances where individuals have a diminished capacity to decide about how to act, their reliance on habits increases. For Wood (2017), habits can shed new light on the question: How can people express intergroup acceptance but practice segregation and discrimination? She suggests that one explanation is that discrimination is often habitual. If discrimination in constant, such behaviours can reflect habitual 'choices' to favour one group over others, allowing prejudice to continue. However, when habits are questioned by the presence of the stranger this can strengthen people's intentions. Discrimination and exclusion may still be present but will not be habitual.

Conclusion

The processes of estrangement are embedded within ordinary everyday social–cognitive processes and practices found in interpersonal as well as intergroup contexts. The argument presented here is that estrangement is a product of social practice through which not only understandings of what it means to be 'strange' are propagated and maintained but people's subjectivities in relation to the stranger are shaped and constructed.

Practice is never owned by a single individual but rather is present in various sets of connections or set of contacts and can be exercised only so far as the individuals are free to choose actions from within a field of possibilities. Although from Schatzki's (2002) perspective practices have a scripted feel, human agents always find the need to engage in a reflexive monitoring of action and the outcome of this reflection can be the basis for our motivation to act. Interaction can be innovative and often disruptive as there are always opportunities for reflection informed by our discursive consciousness. For Giddens, the true measure of a knowledgeable agent is that they 'could have acted otherwise' (Giddens 1982: 9). The conception of 'could have acted otherwise' represents the positive side of practice-based conceptions of the stranger as each of us as human agents has the ability to recursively influence the social processes by which negative forms of estrangement are created. As human agents we have the capacity for critical consciousness and can be agents of change over our own lives and influence the practices used to define the stranger.

References

Baker, G. P.and Hacker, P. M. S.(2009) *Wittgenstein understanding and meaning*, 2nd edn: Volume 1 (Analytical Commentary on the Philosophical Investigations). Oxford:Wiley-Blackwell.

Berger, P. L. and Luckmann, T. (1967) *The social construction of reality; a treatise in the sociology of knowledge*. Harmondsworth: Penguin.

Campbell, D. T. (1963) Attitudes and other acquired behavioural dispositions. In S. Koch (ed.), *Psychology: A study of a science. Study II. Empirical substructure and relations with other sciences. Investigations of man as socius: Their place in psychology and the social sciences* (vol. 6, pp. 94–172). New York, NY: McGraw-Hill.

Cavell, S. (1988) Declining decline: Wittgenstein as a philosopher of culture. *Inquiry*, 31, 253–264.

Conway, G. D. (1989) *Wittgenstein on foundations*. Atlantic Highlands, NJ: Humanities Press.

Garfinkel, H. (1967) *Studies in ethnomethodology*. Cambridge: Polity.

Giddens, A. (1979) *Central problems in social theory: Action, structure, and contradiction in social analysis*. Basingstoke: Palgrave Macmillan.

Giddens, A. (1982) *Profiles and critiques in social theory*. Basingstoke: Macmillan.

James, W. (1890) *Habit*. New York, NY: Henry Holt.

Lingis, A. (1994) *The community of those who have nothing in common*. Bloomington: Indiana University Press.

Loersch, C. and Payne, B. K. (2011) The situated inference model an integrative account of the effects of primes on perception, behavior, and motivation. *Perspectives on Psychological Science*, 6, 234–252.

Marx, K. (1959) Theses on Feuerbach. In L. S. Feuer (ed.), *Marx and Engels: Basic writings on politics and philosophy* (pp. 283–286). New York, NY: Lewis S. Feuer.

Neal, D. T., Wood, W. and Drolet, A. (2013) How do people adhere to goals when willpower is low? The profits (and pitfalls) of strong habits. *Journal of Personality and Social Psychology*, 104, 959–975.

Oakeshott, M. (1975) *On human conduct*. Oxford: Clarendon Press.

Parsons, T. (1937) *The structure of social action: A study in social theory with special reference to a group of recent European writers*. New York: The Free Press.

Reckwitz, A. (2002) Toward a theory of social practices: A development in culturalist theorizing. *European Journal of Social Theory*, 5(2), 243–263.

Schatzki, T. (1997) *Social practices: A Wittgensteinian approach to human activity and the social*. Cambridge: Cambridge University Press.

Schatzki, T. (2002) *The site of the social: A philosophical account of the constitution of social life and change*. University Park: The Pennsylvania State University Press.

Taylor, C. (1985) Interpretation and the sciences of man. In C. Taylor (ed.), *Philosophy and the human sciences: Philosophical papers 2*. Cambridge: Cambridge University Press.

Turner, S. (1994) *The social theory of practices: Tradition, tacit knowledge and presuppositions*. Cambridge: Polity Press.

Wirth, L. (1939) The structure of social action. *American Sociological Review*, 4, 399–404.

Wittgenstein, L. (1972) *On certainty*. New York: Harper Perennial.

Wittgenstein, L. (1978) *Remarks on the foundations of mathematics*, ed. G. H. von Wright, R. Rhees, and G. E. M. Anscombe, trans. G. E. M. Anscombe, revised edn. Oxford: Blackwell.

Wittgenstein, L. (1989) *Wittgenstein's lectures on the foundations of mathematics*, ed. C. Diamond. Chicago: University of Chicago Press.

Wood, W. (2017) Habit in personality and social psychology. *Personality and Social Psychology Review*, 21(4), 389–403.

1

THE CITY

Georg Simmel on the stranger

Georg Simmel's essay *The Stranger* (1908) describes the position of the stranger in social life. Although this essay is only eight pages long, Simmel's reflections on the stranger and metropolitan life continue to influence the ways in which present day commentators think about the political and cultural anxieties that people experience within the urban environment. Simmel identified how the city is still to this day seen as a lifeline for marginal and excluded people. For Simmel, the stranger is not perceived as: 'the wanderer who comes today and goes tomorrow, but rather as the person who comes today and stays tomorrow' (Simmel 1950/1908: 402). The stranger has what Simmel describes as the: 'specific character of mobility' that embodies a 'synthesis of nearness and distance which constitutes the formal position of the stranger' (Simmel 1950/1908: 403–404). The position of the stranger within a group is: 'determined, essentially, by the fact that he has not belonged to it from the beginning, that he imports qualities into it, which do not and cannot stem from the group itself' (Simmel 1950/1908: 402). The position of the stranger stands out more sharply if the stranger settles down in a place, instead of leaving it again. The stranger is supernumerary: 'The stranger is by nature no "owner of soil" soil not only in the physical, but also in the figurative sense of a life-substance which is fixed, if not in a point in space, at least in an ideal point of the social environment' (Simmel 1950/1908: 403). Human beings cannot be defined by their humanity alone, they also have self-definition and an ascribed definition of self, both of which have a central role to play in the formation of identity. Simmel notes that we must not think of the individual 'as a solid substance, but as the peculiar identity of the living with itself' (Pyyhtinen 2012: 82). For Simmel, human beings produce social forms and strangeness is the product of a *form of interaction*; the individual is for Simmel an 'assembled being' (*zusammengesetzte Wesen*) (Simmel 1997a: 323) and the content of our individuality is completely dependent on difference (Simmel 1999: 515). However, the strangeness of the stranger is important in that the perceived difference of the stranger helps to reinforce what the people who describe themselves as 'belonging' have in common. Simmel concludes his essay by suggesting that without the presence of the stranger, social life in the metropolitan money economy would be too uniform and key aspects of self would be diminished.

Simmel is well known as one of the founders of sociology, however he always regarded himself first and foremost as a philosopher. Simmel's philosophical ideas have been largely ignored by sociologists, while philosophers tend to ignore Simmel's contribution to both sociology and philosophy. Simmel's philosophical starting point was an interpretation of Kant which suggests that within our minds there are categories of thought that allow the individual to think in terms of social forms or categories of things, making it possible for individuals to make sense of their experience. However, during a period of rapid social change, such as the rapid urbanisation and industrialisation that Simmel witnessed in Berlin at the end of the nineteenth and early twentieth century, there is the possibility of a degree of incompatibility between the form (the category in our mind) and the (external) content of our experience. Individuals must use the categories of thought or forms to provide thresholds or reasonable parameters that assist the person to make sense of the content of their experiences and observations. Individuals give their experiences meaning by creating categories and boundaries; searching for links between social forms and content to make sense of their experiences in a rapidly changing environment. Without these created boundaries and categories people in the city would experience urban life with much greater meaninglessness and dread. Habits, and the underpinning assumptions upon which they are based, especially if they are shared by people within a community, provide a degree of ontological security.

Simmel accepted David Hume's argument that people are habit-forming by nature. In *An Enquiry Concerning Human Understanding*, Hume (2001) argued that the repetition of an act generates a propensity to renew or repeat the same act in similar circumstances and is the basis of custom. For Simmel social action takes place within a context of Hume's understanding of custom and habit. In her review of the nature and role of habit, Wendy Wood (2017) argues that 'habit mechanisms' sustain self-regulation. It is commonly assumed that when people repeat actions in the same context, the influence of habit increases and the influence of intention decreases. Individuals may impart intentionality onto their habits, mistakenly regarding externally prompted thoughts and understandings as their own choices (Loersch and Payne 2011). Habits guide or influence later behaviour. Wood also explains that William James (1890) believed: 'habit covers a very large part of life' (p. 3) and assumed that habits have an abstract quality and act as a symbolic, conservative force in society. Neal, Wood and Drolet (2013) argue that in circumstances where individuals have a diminished capacity to decide about how to act, their reliance on habits increases. However, habits often become central to practice and can be seen to strengthen as well as diminish individuals' intentions.

The Metropolis and Mental Life

Simmel's contribution to our understanding of the stranger was developed against the backcloth of rapid urbanisation and the rise of the money economy. Based on his own experiences of life in Berlin in the 1890s, looking out from his bedroom window at the corner of Leipzigerstrasse and Friedrichstrasse, *The Metropolis and Mental Life* is something of a personal reflection on the ways in which the metropolitan environment redefined the relations between space, spatial practices and subjectivities. For Simmel: 'The City is not a spatial entity with social consequences, but a sociological entity that is formed spatially' (Simmel 1997: 131). Simmel argued that one of the psychological consequences of rapid urbanisation was a form of disaffection that encouraged estrangement rather than sociability. To protect themselves against this, many metropoles developed a blasé attitude; a new form of subjectivity better suited to the demands of the metropolitan environment.

The metropolis provided the condition for the emergence of cosmopolitanism. In contrast to the 'slower, more habitual, more smoothly flowing rhythm of the sensory-mental phase of small town and rural existence' (Simmel 1972: 325), metropolitan life is capitalistic and intellectualistic in character and the 'tempo' and 'multiplicity of economic, occupational and social life' (Simmel 1972: 325) is very fast. For the modern person, maintaining a degree of independence and individuality in relation to the sovereign powers of society, including our shared sense of historical heritage, culture and accepted ways of leading a life, is described by Simmel as one of the deepest problems of modern life. In the modern world, there is a relationship between the social structure that promotes individuality and at the same time modernity promotes aspects of life that go above and beyond the interests of single individuals.

In Simmel's day, as today the influence of the metropolitan environment reaches well beyond its physical boundaries. The current levels of urbanisation are unprecedented and over the last decade there has been a substantial increase of new migrants into large cities. The link that Simmel identified between the stranger, the city and boundaries still shapes current debates about the stranger. Cities are globally important because they are often in the front line dealing with the problems created by migration. For Bauman (2016) cities are comparable to garbage cans into which all the problems that have emerged from the processes of globalisation have been randomly poured.

Although cities do not follow a single pattern of development, the urban environment is always characterised by a large aggregation and relatively dense concentration of population. Simmel explained how the process of urbanisation and industrialisation generates urban anonymity and impersonality (*gesellschaft*) that is absent from the traditional community. As such, migrants to cities face new challenges that they did not face in traditional communities. In the city people will only know a small number of other residents and, unlike in the village where it was not uncommon for people know each other well, in the city proximity to our neighbours does not assure feelings of community. Rather, ways of living in the city can generate feelings of isolation, separation and insecurity. The urban resident may have contact with many other people but does not get to know many of them well. Disconnection from others and feelings of anonymity are a consequence of the concentration of large numbers of often diverse people in big cities. Life within the city for Simmel was characterised by an ever-expanding diversification of life-spheres and individuals deeply engaged in one life-sphere can find it difficult to speak with other individuals involved in another life-sphere, and as a consequence conflict can occur.

Traditionally, 'place' shaped the identity of its inhabitants; for Simmel the traditional relation between place, communality and identity has been dissolved by the processes of urbanisation. A sense of 'place' is no longer viewed as the foundation of a stable social identity. The experience of the city is subjective, but impacts on state of mind, character and identity of the urban resident. The consciousness of the self and our relation to the Other is both a medium and an outcome of life in the city. As Sabine Buchholz and Manfred Jahn explain: 'space always include a subject who is affected by (and in turn affects) space, a subject who experiences and reacts to space in a bodily way, a subject who "feels" space through existential living conditions, mood, and atmosphere' (Buchholz and Jahn 2005: 553). In Simmel's analysis, the city reflects the dynamic and diverse culture of modernity and generates a new sense of proximity and distance.

In *The Metropolis and Mental Life* Simmel examines the influence of urban life on the psychological and cultural elements of sociality. At the time when Simmel was writing in the nineteenth century, cosmopolitan relations were infrequent and fragile. In the opening sentence Simmel identifies the impact of modernity on the mundane practices of everyday life: 'The deepest problems of modern life derive from the claim of the individual to preserve the autonomy and individuality of his existence' (Simmel 1997b: 409).

The contemporary city is characterised by flows of people, symbols and material goods as the city is interconnected to numerous other places via global-local networks or flows that impact on everyday social practice. As John Allen explains:

> Simmel's thinking on proximity, distance and movement can shed
> light upon how people make sense of today's complex networks of

social interaction both within and beyond cosmopolitan city life ...
modern times for Simmel are experienced largely through changing relations of proximity and distance and, more broadly,
through cultures of movement and mobility.

(Allen 2000: 55)

Our encounters with others, our social and cultural relations are based
upon sets of practices not needed in the rural environment. There is a
newness to the experiences people had in the rapidly expanding nineteenth-century urban surroundings. The city provides meeting places
for different groups and urban space is occupied by people in diverse
ways. The emergence of the *flaneur*, for example was a product of the
urban environment not known in the rural setting, a person who
spends their days wandering around the streets of Paris and other cities
as spectator-traveller, looking at the world and enjoying being exposed
to the gaze of others. For the *flaneur* the city offers a liberating experience. In a similar fashion, Simmel looked at the position of the stranger
as a social construction put together from everyday social practice, in
relation to proximity and interaction.

There is something distinctive about urban sociality; the city is the
central force in shaping individual lives. There is a degree of ambivalence to city life, according to Simmel, in that the city provides
opportunities to act in a way that is free from rural constraints and
expectations. At the same time city life can induce feelings of detachment. The city was associated with a distinctive outlook for Simmel,
the '*blasé* attitude':

The *blasé* attitude results first from the rapidly changing and closely compressed contrasting stimulations of the nerves ... An inca-
pacity thus emerges to react to new sensations with the appropriate
energy. This constitutes that *blasé* attitude which, in fact, every
metropolitan child shows when compared with children of quieter
and less changeable milieus.

(Simmel 1997b: 414)

The degree of ambivalence to city life provides opportunities to act in a
way that is free from constraints and expectations. At the same time city

life can induce feelings of detachment. Simmel's argument has much in common with the themes later explored by Marc Augé's (2002) *In the Metro*, an ethnographic investigation focused on the experience of travelling on the Parisian Metro. City metro systems are more than just a way to get from one place to another, they are often ambiguous spaces. Augé's focus is on the experience of the time and space provided by travelling on the metro. The journey is often taken alone in solitude, often near 'proximal others', people who appear to be like ourselves, the middle classes and the excluded; the metro is a place where we encounter the homeless, beggars and street entertainers.

Influence of Simmel

Levine (1977) rightly points out that Simmel's essay on the stranger was a stimulus to the study of stranger and social distance, including: Robert Park's concept of *Marginal Man*, Paul Siu's concept of the *Sojourner*, Alfred Schütz's concept of the *Homecomer* and Lewis Coser's understanding of the *Alien*. However, Levine also argues that much of the research that took its lead from Simmel, such as viewing the stranger as a 'marginal man', 'the newly arrived outsider' or 'ethnic communities' is based upon a misreading of Simmel's central argument about the links between nearness and remoteness within a bounded group. Simmel's stranger is not a person who attempts to be assimilated into the host community but fails. There are several aspirations that Simmel's stranger may have in relation to the bounded community and several possible responses that the bounded community may have in relation to the stranger.

Park (1928) explains to his reader that he explicitly attempted to base his conception of the marginal man on Simmel's conception of the stranger. The marginal man was defined solely in terms race and ethnicity, and Park regarded the Jew as the prime example of the marginal man. Insecurity and instability were central to the life experience of the marginal man whose marginal personality was a product of the marginal situation that he found himself in. For this reason, the marginal man was attracted to the 'marginal culture' shared by other similarly positioned people to offer some security and protection from discrimination and stigmatisation. The marginal man is defined as an individual who is:

living and sharing intimately in the cultural life and traditions of two distinct peoples, never quite willing to break, even if he were permitted to do so, with his past and his traditions, and not quite accepted, because of racial prejudice, in the new society in which he now seeks to find a place.

(Park 1928: 892)

Taking his starting point from Robert Park (1928), Stonequist (1935) is interested in the precarious lives of mixed-race people who are much more likely to develop into a marginal character. Marginality is an abstraction: 'a core of psychological traits which are the inner correlates of the dual pattern of social conflict and identification' (Stonequist 1935: 10). Stonequist argues that most people live their lives within one cultural tradition, with one set of loyalties to one government, and in compliance with one moral code. However, because of the processes of globalisation and the migration associated with it, many individuals are relocated, together with their cultures, to such a degree that people in the city often find themselves growing up in a: 'more complex and less harmonious cultural situation'. People in the city are often unintentionally socialised into 'two or more historic traditions, languages, political loyalties, moral codes, and religions ... every city is something of a melting-pot of races and nationalities' (Stonequist 1935: 2). Individuals who lead their lives within and between two cultures often develop a 'marginal personality', which involves some cultural conflict and the emergence of what Du Bois called a 'double consciousness': 'double-consciousness, this sense of always looking at one's self through the eyes of others, of measuring one's soul by the tape of a world that looks on in amused contempt and pity' (Du Bois 1903: 3; cited in Stonequist 1935: 7).

Cooley's looking glass self involves looking at ourselves as others see us; imagining the judgement of others and using this judgement in the construction of self. The marginal personality experiences not just the *looking glass self* that Cooley describes, but is: 'placed simultaneously between two looking-glasses' (Stonequist 1935: 7). As such their life-organisation can become acutely disturbed, as the individual can feel as if the two races contained within look at each other and make a judgement. Like Park, Stonequist views the Jew as the typical marginal man; always in the minority and often the 'perennial immigrant': 'Centuries of social conflict, combined with their tenacious historical memories, have produced a group consciousness which in turn suspects and resists assimilation tendencies which go beyond a certain point' (Stonequist 1935: 9).

Although Park's concept of the marginal man and the development of the concept by Stonequist can be read as a very selective reading of Simmel on the stranger, what Park and Stonequist do is to identify the role of racist practice in the process of estrangement and more significantly identify the role of racist practices in the formation of subjectivity. The often failed process of transition from outsider to insider that many strangers go through is what later social commentators were to identify as underpinning the processed of liminality and the precarious life.

Alfred Schütz (1944) views the stranger not as a visitor or guest but as an individual who is seen to be a newcomer, an outsider or migrant who attempts to become accepted by a group but who currently has no status in the eyes of group members. Examples that Schütz gives include the person from the city who moves to a rural community, the bridegroom who attempts to become accepted by the bride's family or the farmer's son who goes to university. The stranger is not acquainted with the common ways of behaving or the common ways of thinking within the group. Drawing on William James (1890) Schütz suggests that the stranger's view of the group is only partially clear and contradictory, and this incoherence is a product of the stranger's lack of 'knowledge of acquaintance' or 'knowledge about' the group. In Max Scheler's terms the stranger cannot engage in thinking *as usual* within the group, the stranger does not yet share the group's relatively natural conception of the world. The culture of the group is not part of the stranger's biography and as such the stranger continues to look at the actions and assumptions of the group from the perspective of their own family background. As such the stranger must define the situation of the group and this provides the stranger with a degree of objectivity because the stranger judges the groups by standards that have been acquired from outside of the group. However, this objectivity also raises questions about the stranger's loyalty to the group. The questioning of the stranger's loyalty to the group manifests itself as prejudice towards strangers; a situation that will continue until the stranger has successfully completed a process of social adjustment or assimilation into the cultural patterns of the group.

Similar themes are also taken up in Schütz's (1972) essay *The Homecomer*, which opens with the account of the return of Odysseus to Ithaca. The sleeping Odysseus is placed by Phaeacian sailors on the shore of his homeland. However, when he awakens he is unsure as to his whereabouts and the place looks unfamiliar. Unlike the stranger, the homecomer does not believe themselves to be a stranger in a strange country; rather the homecomer's attitude is they still have intimate knowledge of the place and of the taken for granted order of things. The returning veteran, the emigrant who returns to their native land, the traveller who comes back from exploring foreign countries, and the boy who 'made good' abroad and returns home are all instances of what Schütz refers to as the 'homecomer'.

The concept of home is emotionally charged yet hard to describe; it means different things to different people but for Schütz 'home' is interpreted as a pure form of togetherness: 'father-house and mother-tongue, the family, the sweetheart, the friends; it means a beloved landscape, 'songs my mother taught me', food prepared in a particular way, familiar things for daily use, folkways, and personal habits' (Schütz 1972: 108). Drawing upon Cooley's (1909) concept of the primary group, to feel at home means to follow a pattern of routine or habit that one is comfortable and familiar with. We know how to react and how others will react to us: 'a peculiar way of life composed of small and important elements' (Schütz 1972: 108). The people who share our home become part of our personal history and help to shape our biography.

To leave home is to adopt other goals from the in-group or other means for attaining them. In the case of soldiers who have had battle field experience, it can arise that the soldier comes to the opinion that people at home do not understand the meaning and significance of the new individual experiences such as the struggle for survival, the fulfilment of a duty, endurance and sacrifice. Experiences away from home, especially if the person was previously not aware of their ability to perform such actions, can change the perspective and the attitude of the homecomer: 'each homecomer has tasted the magic fruit of strangeness, be it sweet or bitter' (Schütz 1972: 116).

The sojourner as described by Paul Siu (1952) also claims to take its point of departure from Simmel. The sojourner is a type of stranger, a foreigner who has spent a long time overseas and away from home but who maintains the 'bi-cultural complex' of the 'marginal man'; a person without the desire to become a permanent resident and who has no wish to assimilate into the culture of the country where they currently reside but rather upholds the culture of their own ethnic group. The sojourner's home culture remains the benchmark or point of reference by which all other cultural forms and practices are judged. The reasons why the sojourner chooses to travel and live overseas are many and varied, however, the motive contains a task – to get a degree, to earn money, to convert people to a religious cause and the intention of the sojourner is to return home as soon as the task is completed.

The sojourner chooses to live near and associate mainly with people from their own ethnic group. Areas of cities where the sojourner lives become connected with ethnicity and a local economy emerges to satisfy the needs to the ethnic group who live there. These areas are often places where in-group contacts are maintained and labelled with names as such Chinatown, Little Italy, etc.

Simmel argues that the stranger 'often receives the most surprising openness-confidences which sometime have the character of a confessional and which would be carefully withheld from more closely related persons' (Simmel 1950/1908: 404). From this premise, and drawing on the examples of the Court Jews of Baroque Germany and the Christian renegades of the Ottoman Empire, Lewis Coser (1972) argues that when political rulers want to maximize their power and autonomy in the face of impediments, they often recruit individuals from alien groups who have no roots in the country. The independence of the alien was based on their distance from the population. In addition, as their position was insecure and marginal, the rootless alien was an ideal servant of power as the alien outsider was often totally dependent on the ruler; in that the position of the alien depended wholly on the personal support of the ruler. The effectiveness of the relationship rested on mutual confidence and mutual support.

The city as a lifeline

The escalation of international migration of refugees and asylum see-kers in the twenty-first century took governments and citizens by surprise. In addition, once flows began, governments experienced great difficulty controlling these flows. Migratory flows are often involuntary, made up of people who are victims of conflict in their home countries. Such people make their way to the city out of des-peration. The city is seen as a lifeline providing shelter in which to survive for many international migrants who have lost everything. The city offers the migrant necessities such as food and temporary accommodation, and an opportunity to maintain a form of solidarity with other people who share the same fate.

Before having the status of 'forced migrant' imposed upon them, many of these individuals lived normal, respectable lives in their own community, with employment, a secure identity and a degree of eco-nomic security. However, because of factors outside of their immediate control these individuals rapidly and unexpectedly find themselves without financial resources, anonymous, unprotected, homeless, state-less and stripped of their dignity and humanity.

For the so-called 'economic migrant', the city is seen as a place where you can have a better life; a lively and vibrant place that provides economic opportunities that do not exist in rural areas or in their home countries. Cities provide employment opportunities even for people with no marketable skills and abilities as there is a strong demand for services from unskilled workers.

Migration is no longer an issue that affects only the remote regions of the globe; the processes of globalisation allow flows of anonymous, disposed people to arrive at our shores. Migrants make their way to the city where they are often viewed with suspicion and distrust. However, the city is a place in which it is easier to find shelter and survive, although marginalisation is often the price to pay for making that choice. Although conflict, persecution and trafficking are important causes of migration, significant numbers of migrants also move for economic reasons. For the so-called 'economic migrant', the city is seen as a lively and vibrant place that provides opportunities that do not exist in rural areas or in their home countries.

Cosmopolitanism brings about a transformation of everyday life. Ulrich Beck is often assumed to present cosmopolitanism as a product of greater sociocultural interaction between people across national borders and the view that, because of globalisation, people tend to treat others from outside the national border with greater openness than they did in the past. However, national citizenship remains the central defining aspect of 'difference' and access to economic resources and access to social and political rights remain rooted in national citizenship. As such, boundaries around 'difference' can become deeply contested, generating forms of exclusion rooted in racism and violence and, in some cases, such as the 7/7 London bombers, related to global conflicts, such as the role of the United States and United Kingdom in military interventions. *Cosmopolitanisation* is then the dark side of cosmopolitanism and the negative impact of cosmopolitanisation can be observed in aspects of city life. Cosmopolitanism then does not replace nationalist sentiments in a zero-sum manner; rather cosmopolitanism is a dialectical process that comes into being when nationalism is also present (Beck 2002: 39). As Beck and Sznaider make clear: 'Cosmopolitanism does not only negate nationalism but also presupposes it' (Beck and Sznaider 2006: 20).

People may live near each other, but they often ignore and fail to communicate with each other. Individuals can become more distant, despite living next to each other in the same city. The detached and silent acceptance of false integration provides the basis for the more odious condition of cosmopolitanisation. Cosmopolitanisation often presents itself as demands for the nation state to curb immigration and prevent the migratory flows of refuges and asylum seekers from crossing our borders.

In Simmel's analysis the metropolis is dominated by the money economy and a *matter-of-fact* attitude towards persons and things, what Simmel calls the 'domination of the intellect'. In the metropolis money is used to define something that is common to all persons and all things. Exchange value is used to reduce all quality and individuality to a numerical quantitative level. Accepting the importance of exchange value in terms of monetary value allows the modern person to view very different things in terms of one common element. Modern people can become indifferent to every other aspect of persons and things except the objectively perceivable monetary value of that thing or person. All aspects of metropolitan life can become reduced to exact monetary equivalents. Money becomes the common denominator of all values. Viewing all things in terms of monetary equivalents erases all other qualitative distinctions. In Simmel's view, society is the product of the processes of association brought about by individual people interacting with each other and attempting to achieve what they feel is in their own best interests. To protect the self from the possible negative impact of metropolitan life, the modern mind has become much more calculating. In many respects, Simmel's conception of metropolitan life has much in common with Michael Serres's (1982) conception of the parasite relationship. Serres's (1982) central argument is that the relationship between a parasite and host is useful for understanding the basis of all intersubjectivity. Serres replaces Marx's concept of 'exchange value' with the concept of 'abuse value', which he describes as a one-directional, 'complete, irrevocable consummation'. Abuse value 'precedes use and exchange-value' because 'exchange is always weighed, measured, calculated, taking into account a relation without exchange, an abusive relation' (Serres 1982: 80). At the origin of human society, we find the parasitic logic of taking without giving; 'abuse value' comes before 'use value'. This suggests that there are two overlapping conceptions of the stranger in Simmel: on the one hand the stranger who is welcomed because of the services that can offer the community and on the other hand those strangers who are regarded as skilled and seen to offer little to community life.

Modern people who are successful in the metropolis develop an 'intellectualistic quality' or the 'domination of the intellect'. Simmel argues that this *blasé* outlook provides some protection to the inner life of the people against the domination of the metropolis. The *blasé* attitude is not only indifference towards other people but is rooted in a mutual strangeness. The metropolitan life generates a type of culture in which the personality can barely maintain itself. The metropolitan person can come to feel 'atomised internally', as the culture of metropolitan life slowly draws the personality downward into a feeling of its own valuelessness. This leads to a specifically metropolitan need for self-esteem achieved by making oneself noticeable, to be seen to be different through eccentricities and extravagances. Not always successfully. Our inner unity and the reciprocal interactions and interconnections with others are weakened: 'one never feels as lonely and as deserted as in this metropolitan crush of persons' (Simmel 1997b: 73).

The stranger is then seen as a person who does not share the common features of established group members. The stranger, Simmel explains is 'fixed within a group whose boundaries are similar to spatial boundaries' (Simmel 1950/1908: 402–403). The stranger is not necessarily committed to the distinctive habits, tastes or preferences of the group, and can have an attitude of 'objectivity' towards the group and its activities. The stranger does not feel bound by the group and has no commitments to the group or to maintaining what makes the group distinct from other groups. As such the stranger is freer, both practically and theoretically, than recognised members of the group.

Strangeness can also be a source of epistemological privilege and neutrality, hence we find reference in Simmel to the stranger as arbitrator and interpreter. The stranger can often also play the role of confidant a person who: 'receives the most surprising revelations and confidences, at times reminiscent of a confessional, about matters which are kept carefully hidden from everybody with whom one is close' (Simmel 1971a: 145). In addition, because of the lack of opportunities to engage in employment as a paid employee, strangers often find themselves by necessity having to engage in trade or working independently, for example in the financial sector. Simmel explains that the position of the stranger allows them to take on the role of the trader in societies as they are often in a stronger position to source goods that are produced outside the community: 'In the whole history of economic activity the stranger makes his appearance everywhere as a trader, and the trader makes his as a stranger' (Simmel 1971a: 144).

However, in a fashion not wholly dissimilar to Emmanuel Levinas, for Simmel there is an ethical dimension to sociability that is focused on the care of the Other or care of the stranger. All people have an element of human commonness because they are recognised as 'people'. It is this recognition of human commonness as a person that provides the stranger with a sense of nearness to the group but at the same there a distance in the quality of the relationship between the stranger and the group. There are aspects or non-common elements possessed by the stranger which emphasise that this person is a stranger to the country.

The non-common element that the stranger possesses is not viewed by the group as a distinct, individual characteristic, but merely as a trait that is common to many strangers: 'For this reason, strangers are not really conceived as individuals, but as strangers of a particular type' (Simmel 1950/1908: 407).

The simplest structures to be found in social interactions take place between two individuals, what Simmel describes as the dyad. Within the dyad there is a different relation between the members from those found in larger groups. For Simmel two people have a 'peculiar close-ness' that is disrupted by the presence of a third person, which he terms the triad or 'the third element'. In addition to the direct relationship between one person and one other, the presence of the third introduces an indirect relationship: 'No matter how close a triad may be, there is always the occasion on which two of the three members regard the third as an intruder ... the sensitive union of two is always irritated by the spectator' (Simmel 1950: 135–136). The presence of the third introduces a 'social framework', suggests Simmel. Again, in a similar fashion to Emmanuel Levinas, Simmel argues that: 'the triad is a struc-ture completely different from the dyad but not, on the other hand, specifically distinguished from groups of four or more members' (Simmel 1950: 141).

Observations about the moral party of two being disrupted by the presence of the third have been developed by several authors, notably Emmanuel Levinas, but also Knud Løgstrup and Martin Buber. All three of these authors are concerned with the ways in which we should engage with the stranger ethically. These approaches are more fully explored in Chapter 3 on Zygmunt Bauman and the stranger.

Practice is central to Simmel's understanding of the construction of social life; interaction is the process that generates social life. In Sim-mel's view, social life is the outcome of the practices that underpin the associations that individuals draw upon whilst interacting with each other. As Simmel (1971) explains, in European languages the word 'society' indicates plainly and simply 'togetherness' underpinned by a form of sociability, which in its pure form 'has no ulterior end, no content, and no result outside itself'. In the same way that energy impacts on atoms to bring matter into being as tangible 'things'. The same is also the case, argues Simmel, with the impulses and interests of people; underpinning content-determined concreteness of association, individuals experience impulses and the need to fulfil their interests, which pushes people towards one another and brings about forms of association. Sociability is the abstraction of association. Although association can be felt as a burden, or something to be tolerated, an association with others in any form is accompanied by feelings of satisfaction because we are doing things with others; a form of togetherness rooted in an impulse to sociability. Self-regulation, tact, unrestrained individuality and aggressiveness are all ingrained in a desire to protect sociability and pure humanity. There is an underpinning democratic structure to all sociability, argues Simmel.

Simmel takes his starting point from Kant's position that 'everyone should have that measure of freedom which could exist along with the freedom of every other person' (Simmel 1949: 257). The principle of sociability is formulated by Simmel in the following terms: 'everyone should guarantee to the other that maximum of sociable values (joy, relief, vivacity) which is consonant with the maximum of values he himself receives' (Simmel 1949: 257). As such, when we 'act' in relation to another, we should do so as though we are both equal parties in the association; to do otherwise is to act in a way that lacks 'the ethical imperative'.

For Simmel individuals are the bearers of the processes of association that form society. Simmel also suggests that all individuals have an impulse to sociability and society is a sociological structure that corresponds to the processes of association that all individuals maintain. All association contains in part a degree of pure sociability. Pure sociability in its pure form has no content outside of itself: 'the impulse to sociability distils as it were, out of the realities of social life the pure essence of association, of the associative process as a value and satisfaction' (Simmel 1949: 255). Moreover, society means togetherness for Simmel and the sociability impulse is the source and substance of sociability that everyone should help to maintain and guarantee. The processes of sociability are focused on reciprocity, the interaction between people as equals and a concern for humanity and not for individual moods, character or other expressions of individuality. For this reason, forms of association that lack reciprocity are regarded as falling short of an ethical imperative. The drive to sociability is the ethical force of concrete society and a symbol of life.

In Simmel's analysis of the stranger, the categories of *strangerhood* and estrangement are sometimes expressed as a category of *constructed otherness*. Alternatively, Simmel also sees the origin of strangeness in relation to a person being classed as 'foreign'. Spatial relations and spatial boundaries are a 'condition' and a 'symbol' of human relations for Simmel and he describes the formal position of the stranger as a synthesis of nearness and distance but also indifference and involvement. The stranger is then not 'organically connected', through kinship or locality with the community and is seen to be 'inorganically appended' to the group. The stranger is seen by the 'more organically connected persons' as having a non-common element, which provides the stranger with the status of a person *in* the group but not wholly *of* the group. There is then a reciprocal tension between the stranger and the group that has a morally lacking aspect.

Simmel explains that the stranger is characterised by a unity of wandering and fixation, a unity of nearness and remoteness; the stranger is a person viewed as a potential wanderer. However, as we have seen, unlike the wanderer who comes today and goes tomorrow, the stranger is a person who comes today and stays tomorrow. The position of the stranger within the group is fixed within a symbolic set of human relations that are like spatial boundaries found in geographical places. Estrangement is the identification of a non-common element in the Other. The non-common element can be associated with a positive or negative evaluation of the Other identified with this element. As such, estrangement is found in the relationships between individuals and in the relationship between individuals and groups. It is because the stranger is always *in* the group but not viewed as being *of* the group that a form of distance is created, which allows the stranger to view the group with a degree of objectivity that 'owners of the soil' do not possess. The stranger has a degree of freedom to view the group and their ways of behaving without prejudice because the stranger has had to make a conscious effort to learn the habits of the group; and for this reason strangers do not view the culture of groups as the only way of organising social life.

Bridge and door

For Simmel the concepts of boundary and border are central to the understanding of social life. The concept of boundary is not only physical for Simmel; boundary is related to the structure of social life, in that boundaries provide arrangements for interaction and making sense of experience. For Simmel, it is not spatial or physical boundaries that influence the communication between individuals and potentially generate conflict between groups, but vice versa: 'the boundary is not a spatial fact with sociological consequences, but a sociological fact that forms itself spatially' (Simmel 1997: 142). Border is a line in space but it also has a psychological and sociological meaning in terms of social demarcation, providing both clarity and security. The border is used to include and to exclude the Other and is a conceptual device for defining the Other as the stranger. As Simmel suggests: 'Wherever the interests of two elements are concerned with the same object, the possibility of their coexistence depends on a boundary line within the object separating their spheres, whether a conflict ends with the establishment of a legal boundary or perhaps begins with a boundary that separates powers' (Simmel 2007: 54).

When people live near to each other, individuals make 'psychological hypotheses' about each other. The *individual stranger* may be personally unknown to us, but *strangers* are known to us. *We* know about people like *them*. In Simmel's view people have a need to construct what they consider may be the motives and intentions of the Other and speculate on how their being there and their possible future actions will impact upon us. To do this people speculate about the 'intimacies and secrecies' of the Other, so that we can feel a sense of intelligibility and security. It is this process of psychological construction about the Other that allows us to define and understand the Other as a: 'unified human being whom we can understand and count on' (Simmel 2007: 54). As individuals, we need this information about the Other so that we can work out how to fulfil our own inner needs and achieve a satisfying practical life. It is based on this information that the 'precarious objective boundary' between self and Other is constructed.

Boundaries help to: establish rights and duties within the collective; define who is a full member of the collective and who is granted only partial membership; establish who should be regarded as fully integrated into the collective and who should not. However, in some cases an individual may feel that they are a full participant in the collective, but the collective limits the degree of participation and views the person as having only partial membership. Although membership of the collective is strictly demarcated, it is not possible to make a quantitative judgement about the division between full and partial member. To be a partial member, argues Simmel, is to have a well-marked role in relation to the collective. This is not a weaker relationship to the totality but involves having a more objective and clearly defined position and a more precise definition of the person's role within the collective and what is expected of the person within that role. The mutual boundary is understood to be rooted in the acceptance of a common set of interests and values; and the partial member is understood not to fully conform to that common set of interest and values.

The meaning and significance of the boundary was also explored in Simmel's essay, *Bridge and Door* (Simmel 1994/1909). As no two objects can share the same space, in the physical world a unity of diversity is not possible. In the social world the ability to connect and separate is something we take for granted. In the natural world everything can be seen to stand in some form of relation to everything else. Natural things are both separated but at the same time connected within a cosmos. However, some things can be conceived to have been displaced or removed from a given space and no one thing can share the same space as another thing. As people, we are bordering creatures who can conceptually connect and separate; we are, according to Simmel, connecting creatures who connect but cannot connect without separating. However, we can only make a connection between things if we previously assumed that they were separate and at the same time we can only separate things if it was previously assumed that they were connected. Our ability to connect things that were previously seen to be separate is reflected in our ability to construct paths and bridges. Path building is a distinct human achievement. However, the building of a bridge is an even greater human achievement in overcoming space to facilitate connectivity. The bridge identifies anchor points and connects them around a single meaning. The direction of travel along the bridge does not make a difference in terms of the meaning of the act. In contrast, the door forms a linkage between a space for human beings and everything else from nature that remains outside and as such the door represents in a more decisive manner how separating and connecting are two sides of the same act. The door transcends inner and outer, representing both separation and connection; the door provides isolation and represents a boundary. Whereas the bridge provides direction between a finite place and another finite place; the door provides security but not direction. Unlike the window, which has much less significance in terms of transcending inner and outer, life flows in any direction from the open door. Doors symbolise the movement of life from inside to outside and from outside to inside. The underpinning ideas in Bridge and Door have been more fully developed in Zygmunt Bauman's *Strangers at our Door* (Bauman 2016), which will be explored in Chapter 3. In addition, other authors have also drawn upon the ideas that Simmel expressed, notably Jacques Derrida.

Derrida (2000), for example, draws upon Simmel's ideas on bridge and door in his analysis of hospitality. Derrida, like Simmel, also opens his account of hospitality with a passage from Kant who argues that hospitality is a 'cosmopolitan right' not rooted in either morality or politics but citizenship. All citizens have a human right to hospitality:

> [H]ospitality means the right of a stranger not to be treated as an enemy when he arrives in the land of another. One may refuse to receive him when this can be done without causing his destruction, but so long as he peacefully occupies his place, one may not treat him with hostility. [...] it is only a right of temporary sojourn that all men have as a right to associate by virtue of their common possession of the surface of the earth, where, as a globe, they cannot infinitely disperse and hence must finally tolerate the presence of each other. Originally, no one had more right than another to a particular part of the earth.
>
> *(Kant 1957/1795: 20)*

Hospitality is the opposite of hostility. Hospitality is not something that people 'owe'; it is a question of welcoming the stranger. The stranger has the right not to be treated with hostility when they arrive in someone else's territory. The stranger should be treated as a welcome

guest and not an enemy. However, this is not an unconditional welcome. Drawing upon the metaphor of the door, Derrida argues that
when we receive the stranger and welcome them through the door, it
is on condition that the stranger behaves in the way that we regard as
customary that we give asylum but maintain authority. Hospitality is
then for Derrida a self-contradictory concept in that it contains conditions that are imposed upon the stranger. The stranger has no rights
beyond the ones given by the host or 'acceptor'. Hospitality is always
conditional, and the state determines the limits to hospitality:

> [F]or there to be hospitality, there must be a door. But if there is a
> door, there is no longer hospitality there is no hospitable house.
> There is no house without doors and windows. But as soon as there
> are a door and windows, it means that someone has the key to them
> and consequently controls the conditions of hospitality. There must
> be a threshold. But if there is a threshold, there is no longer hospi-
> tality. This is the difference, the gap, between the hospitality of
> invitation and the hospitality of visitation. In visitation there is no
> door. Anyone can come at any time and can come in without
> needing a key for the door. There are no customs checks with a
> visitation. But there are customs and police checks with an invita-
> tion. Hospitality thus becomes the threshold or the door.
>
> *(Derrida 2000: 14)*

Hospitality contains within itself the very opposite of what it claims to
be. Hospitality is the thing that defines who can and cannot cross the
threshold and it is the thing that is used to define a person as a stranger.
It is hospitality that is used to identify place of birth as the central
characteristic of the stranger. Above all else, we know the stranger by
where the person comes from.

Life as transcendence

In his essay *Life as Transcendence* (Simmel 2010/1918) Simmel more
fully explains that as people we find ourselves living our lives within
boundaries that we use to continually position ourselves and find
direction within our social worlds. Boundaries set the limits of ordinary

experience. Our understanding of the content of our lives stands in relation to these boundaries. However, in contrast to the view that boundaries reflect *a priori* categories, Simmel argues that although we may experience the boundaries as constraining, they are created by us the individuals who are constrained by them. As Simmel makes clear: 'Along with the fact that we have boundaries always and everywhere, so also we are boundaries' (Simmel 2010/1918: 1).

Individual people are the carriers and creators of borders and boundaries. For Simmel, individual people inevitably create limits and the conditions for transcending those limits. Individual people define themselves and set the limits of themselves internally from their own perspective. This process of defining self progresses spatially to the point where the individual feels comfortable with a locality that they come to define as their environment. However, external events can always encroach on a person's life in a way that encourages the person to redefine the world and their place within it.

Simmel describes individuals as: 'closed, self-centred, unambiguously distinct beings' (Simmel 2010/1918: 9). Metaphysically this reflects what Simmel describes as the 'problematic condition of life': on the one hand we view life as a boundless continuity but, at the same time, each one of us has a boundary-determined personality. Furthermore, whatever we experience in life we recreate that experience as something that is bounded in order to understand it. As people we live in a border region; at the same time as individuals we can imagine that there might be something in the world that we cannot think of. For Simmel this represents the ability of the mental life to think beyond itself; to think beyond the boundary, an act of self-transcendence.

Life is then experienced as being both objectively bounded and subjectivity free: 'the innermost essence of life is its capacity to go out beyond itself, to set its limits by reaching out beyond them; that is, beyond itself' (Simmel 2010/1918: 10). From Simmel's perspective, each of us is then capable of self-change. Simmel views life in terms of what he describes as life having 'more-life', or 'more-than-life'. 'More' is the ability of the person to draw something into themselves to transform themselves, to grow, to move beyond their current boundedness and create a life. Life stretches out towards nothingness. Simmel understands agency as the 'I', the knowing consciousness, the living human spirit or self-awareness that includes the intellectual process of subjectivisation, a practical self-appraisal, by which the individual confronts itself, looking at self as a third party would look at self and recreating self and identity.

The stranger is not understood as an unfamiliar person but in terms of absoluteness of the stranger's otherness. The stranger is the Other who is not like us. Agency is central to Simmel's understanding of the stranger; we create boundaries, culture and our sense of self. As such, no boundary is unconditional, and every boundary can be 'stepped over' or displaced, although by doing so we inevitably find ourselves creating a new boundary. Despite this, many of us are unaware that our ways of living are constrained within boundaries or that we are the architects and the boundary builders, let alone that boundaries can be stepped over or displaced. Moreover, even people who recognise that they can step outside of a given boundary are concerned that the unforeseen consequences of choosing to step over a boundary may have damaging effects on us. For Simmel we stand in *the between* of knowing and not-knowing: 'we are bounded in every direction, and we are bounded in no direction' (Simmel 2010/1918: 2).

Boundaries are important in Simmel's analysis and all social interaction can be located on a scale from closeness to remoteness; the public and private spaces of social life. The stranger is someone who stands outside of the boundary we impose upon ourselves; as such they have a remoteness and can often recognise the existence of the boundary when we are unaware of a boundary at all. Even when we are aware of the existence of a boundary, many of us do not regard the boundary as constructed by us as an organising principle of how to lead a life but as 'given', as normal and as the natural way of behaving within a given circumstance.

How is society possible?

Simmel's understanding of the stranger is a product of his wider theorising in relation to border, social form and *the third*. These concepts should not be understood in isolation; the concept of the form is a central theoretical and methodological instrument for understanding in Simmel's work. Reality is socially constructed for Simmel and we make sense of the world and the objects of our experience by reference to a form or forms; with a form understood as an epistemological category, a category that allows us to make our experiences intelligible. The form is then the media through which social order is objectified. Social construction is then a subjective process for Simmel that takes place within the consciousness of the individual and is made sense of by reference to forms. As we have seen above, from a Kantian perspective our understanding of the world is constituted by fundamental categories or *a prioris*. The structure of our intellect establishes form, which allows us to make sense of our experience of the world. The categories of the mind are prior to our experience of the world and are the epistemological foundation upon which experience rests. Culture is formed by the categories of the mind. For Simmel, Kantian categories bring about a passive sensibility that is separate from the activity of the constituting subject. When something we come across is familiar to us we can easily place it into a given category and it is said to have 'form' and the meaning has a taken for granted quality; if something we come across is not familiar to us that thing exists and still is regarded as having 'content' but that content does not have a taken for granted quality and needs to be placed into a category. If there is no obvious category in which the content of a thing can be placed, then we must search for one.

Our intellect assembles, orders and forms the content of our sense perceptions. Through the activity of the mind we can transform content into a coherent form; our intellect gives us the ability to fashion content into cognitive categories that have the feel of fixed regularities. Our understanding of the world is then brought into existence by the mind. It is the categories of the mind that allow us to comprehend the things that we observe. Truth is established by the building up of an ideal system of completed cognitions or social categories that people are socialised into. These cognitions and categories are what gives the world form. Individuals also have a 'practical attitude' that allows us to observe 'content' and place it into what we consider to be the appropriate category. This process is also true in terms of the way we engage in the categorising of people. We take elements of the person that we can recognise and use that information to place the unique individual into a category of person:

> We posit every man, with especial bearing upon our practical attitude toward him, as that type of man to which his individuality makes him belong. We think him, along with all his singularity, only under the universal category which does not fully cover him to be sure, and which he does not fully cover.
>
> *(Simmel 1910: 379)*

For Simmel we have little or no choice in the way we look at people. We always see a person as both an individual with a distinct personality and as part of a wider category of person or as part of a group. Often, we engage in this practice when we have only fragmentary data about the individual. We do this to create composite people, so that we know how to relate to people when we have very little information about them. It is this transformation of information about unique individuals into categories of people whom we are confident in terms of how we should behave towards them that brings 'empirical society' into being. Simmel describes this process as a *social apriori*.

> We see the other person not simply as an individual, but as colleague or comrade or fellow partisan; in a word, inhabitant of the same peculiar world.
>
> *(Simmel 1910: 380)*

> This fact operates as social apriori in so far as the part of the individual which is not turned toward the group, or is not dissolved in it, does not lie simply without meaning by the side of his socially significant phase, is not a something external to the group, for which it *nolens volens* affords space; but the fact that the individual, with respect to certain sides of his personality, is not an element of the group, constitutes the positive condition for the fact that he is such a group member in other aspects of his being.
>
> *(Simmel 1910: 381)*

Many cities such as Berlin experienced rapid urbanisation at the end of the nineteenth century and Simmel viewed the city as having a degree of instability to the extent that not all aspects of reality could be readily defined by and assigned to a given category. Social change brings with it new potentialities and energies that Simmel describes as 'more than life', new and different ways of associating, new and different ways of living that were not encountered in the rural environment or in the earlier phases of urbanisation. Simmel conceived of people as competent human agents and he introduces the concept of the *threshold* to describe the situation in which we search for meaning and attempt the categorisation of an object before us. Attempting to make sense of a challenging work of art, for example, involves us looking for limits, dimensions and other qualities to allow categorisation and make the object meaningful or, in Simmel's terms, to give it *form*.

- The threshold is a mental act in which we consciously attempt to ascribe significance by placing an object within a given category but have difficulty doing so.
- The threshold describes the maximum and minimum interpretation of an object; to what extent is the object in front of me like or not like other objects that I am familiar with?
- When an object is beyond the threshold; the threshold is a device for informing us that we must find another way of making something meaningful when it is beyond a given category.

The third

Simmel's conception of the stranger is then contained within a wider understanding of intersubjectivity and the Other. The stranger is conceived by Simmel to be the third. The presence of the third both facilitates social life by reminding 'us' that we have much in common but at the same time disrupts the relationships between 'us'. The presence of the third means that we come to understand that there is the possibility of a third-party perspective and it is the understanding of a third-party perspective that we do not share, but that we are aware of and that allows us to compare individuals in terms of characteristics that we feel we do or do not share with them. The third allows us to look at people in terms of people who are included and people who are excluded. A conception of the third allows us to construct an 'outer' to our social world; a barrier or border. The stranger is not then a role but a configuration of the Other in our imagination. It is this conception of difference or alterity in the imagination that is at the foundation of our identity and subjectivity.

When two people are alone together they can devise ways of behaving that are personal, unique to them and that they feel comfortable with. In addition, those ways of behaving may become habitual. Such ways of behaving may be forms of behaviour that the two people alone would not want others to observe or even be aware of. The third is a transindividual perspective that makes possible self and social understanding. The third is that generalised attitude that we feel a third party may have towards the way we behave when we are out of sight with one other individual. The third provides a link between personal interaction and more formal rule-, convention- or judgement-based external organisation or association. It is for this reason that the third is both internal to the group and external to the group and why the third is viewed as a person we do not know but whom we regard as impartial and whose attitude towards us is always of special concern. The third is then a marginal character but also a central character in that it is the conception of the third that facilitates a critical form of self-reflection that also helps the individual to understand the totality because they have an abstract awareness of social harmony. For Simmel the construction of our subjectivity and our personal and social identity depends on intersubjectivity and the practices of everyday life experiences.

The stranger is central to our understanding of self, society and the Other. Strangers remind us that we live within boundaries. The stranger is not a role that certain people play within the urban environment; the encounter with a stranger is a theatrical encounter:

> The place where we encounter the Stranger is a threshold. Quite literally, I might greet a stranger who comes to my door, and in that space and time discern something about this potential guest. Metaphorically, we can see 'thresholds' defining the edges of human being in many ways: for example, I find a threshold at the limits of my physical body, a threshold of pain, of pleasure, a threshold at the limits of one culture and another, one political group and another.
>
> *(Kearney and Semonovitch 2010: 4)*

The stranger is then never completely external to the group. The presence of the individual that we choose to categorise as not like us and beyond the boundary of the category that we feel we belong to is a resource that we draw upon to produce 'empirical society': 'societary structures are composed of beings who are at the same time inside and outside of them' (Simmel 1910: 390).

It is possible to draw a parallel between Simmel's conception of the form and the third and Berger and Luckmann's social construction of society. Society has something of a phenomenological structure for Simmel that is only discernible through the practice of interacting with and experiencing other individuals. Society is understood by Simmel as an 'objective' reality, produced by social action and a 'subjective' reality. In 'How Is Society Possible?', Simmel (1910) addresses the same question that Berger and Luckmann address: 'How is it possible that subjective meanings become objective facticities?' (Berger and Luckmann 1967: 30).

Also in a similar fashion to Berger and Luckmann, Simmel investigates the intricate ways in which reality is socially constructed, and he shares Berger and Luckmann's opinion that:

> It will be enough, for our purposes, to define 'reality' as a quality appertaining to phenomena that we recognize as having a being independent of our volition (we cannot 'wish them away'), and to define 'knowledge' as the certainty that phenomena are real and that they possess specific characteristics.
>
> *(Berger and Luckmann 1967: 13)*

Conclusion

Georg Simmel's influential essay *The Stranger* (Simmel 1950/1908) describes the position of the stranger in social life. For Simmel, the stranger is not: 'the wanderer who comes today and goes tomorrow, but rather as the person who comes today and stays tomorrow' (Simmel 1950/1908: 402). Although this essay is only eight pages long, Simmel's reflections on the stranger and metropolitan life are widely known and continue to influence the ways in which commentators think about the political and cultural anxieties within the urban environment. The city is still to this day seen as a lifeline for marginal and excluded people and Simmel's concept of the stranger is found in much of the research into a range of different forms of social exclusion. However, the impact of his understanding of the stranger is not straightforward. This chapter looked at Simmel's influence, but his underpinning theoretical perspective is often misunderstood. The stranger is not an object; the presence of the stranger is an integral part of people's interactions within the community. The chapter focused on Simmel's conceptualisation of proximity, distance and the connections between the individual and society that he identified; and commented on the influence of his ideas on generations of theorists and researchers from Robert Park's (1928) *Human Migration and the Marginal Man* through to Zygmunt Bauman's (2016) *Strangers at Our Door*. For Simmel the stranger is then never completely external to the group. The individual experiences society as both an objective that is external to the person and subjective reality; we internalise social forms through a process of socialisation and these allow us to make sense of our subjective experiences and configure our own subjective interpretation. As such the stranger is central to our understanding of self, society and the Other. Strangers remind us that we live within boundaries.

References

Allen, J. (2000) On Georg Simmel: Proximity, distance and movement, in M. Crang and N.Thrift (eds), *Thinking space* (pp. 54–70). London: Routledge.

Augé, M. (2002) *In the metro*. Minneapolis: University of Minnesota Press.

Bauman, Z. (2016) *Strangers at our door*. Cambridge: Polity.

Beck, U. (2002) The cosmopolitan society and its enemies. *Theory, Culture and Society*, 19(1/2), 17–44.

Beck, U. and Sznaider, N. (2006) Unpacking cosmopolitanism for the social sciences: A research agenda. *British Journal of Sociology*, 57(1), 1–23.

Berger, P. and Luckmann, T. (1967) *The social construction of reality; a treatise in the sociology of knowledge*. New York: Doubleday.

Buchholz, S. and Jahn, M. (2005) Space in narrative. In D. Herman, M. Jahn and M-L. Ryan (eds), *Routledge encyclopedia of narrative theory* (pp. 551–555). London: Routledge.

Cooley, C. H. (1909) *Social organization: A study of the larger mind*. New York: John Scribner's Sons.

Coser, L. A. (1972) The alien as a servant of power: Court Jews and Christian renegades. *American Sociological Review*, 37(5), 574–558.

Derrida, J. (2000) Hospitality. *Angelaki*, 5, 3–18.

Hume, D. (2001) *An enquiry concerning human understanding*. The Harvard classics. New York: P. F. Collier and Son.

James, W. (1890) *Habit*. New York: Henry Holt.

Kant, I. (1957/1795). *Perpetual peace* (trans. L. Beck). New York: Liberal Arts Press.

Kearney, R. and Semonovitch, K. (2010) At the threshold: Foreigners, strangers, others. In R. Kearney and K. Semonovitch (eds), *Phenomenologies of the stranger: Between hostility and hospitality* (pp. 3–29). New York: Fordham University Press.

Levine, D. (1977) Simmel at a distance: On the history and systematics of the sociology of the stranger. *Sociological Focus*, 10(1), 15–29.

Loersch, C. and Payne, B. K. (2011) The situated inference model an integrative account of the effects of primes on perception, behavior, and motivation. *Perspectives on Psychological Science*, 6, 234–252.

Neal, D. T., Wood, W. and Drolet, A. (2013) How do people adhere to goals when willpower is low? The profits (and pitfalls) of strong habits. *Journal of Personality and Social Psychology*, 104, 959–975.

Park, R. E. (1928) Human migration and the marginal man. *American Journal of Sociology*, 33(6), 881–893.

Pyyhtinen, O. (2012) Life, death and individuation: Simmel on the problem of life itself. *Theory, Culture and Society*, 29(7–8), 78–100.

Schütz, A. (1944) The stranger: An essay in social psychology. *The American Journal of Sociology*, 49(6), 499–507.

Schütz, A. (1972) The homecomer. In A. Brodersen (Ed.), *Phaenomenologica: Collected papers ll: Studies in Social Theory* (pp. 106–119). The Hague: Martinus Nijhoff.

Serres, M. (1982) *The parasite*. Baltimore, MD: Johns Hopkins University Press.

Simmel, G. (1910) How is society possible? *American Journal of Sociology*, 16(3), 372–391.

Simmel, G. (1949) The sociology of sociability, translated by Everett Hughes. *American Journal of Sociology*, 55(3), 254–261.

Simmel, G. (1950) The isolated individual and the dyad. In K. Wolf (ed.), *The sociology of Georg Simmel* (pp. 135–144). Glenco: The Free Press.

Simmel, G. (1950/1908) The stranger. In K. Wolf (ed.), *The sociology of Georg Simmel* (pp. 401–408). Glenco: The Free Press.

Simmel, G. (1971) Sociability. In D. Levine (ed.), *Georg Simmel on individuality and social forms* (pp. 127–140). Chicago: University of Chicago Press.

Simmel, G. (1971a) Social types. In D. Levine (ed.), *Georg Simmel on individuality and social forms*. Chicago: University of Chicago Press.

Simmel, G. (1972) The metropolis and mental life, in D. Levine (ed.), *Georg Simmel on individuality and social forms*. Chicago: University of Chicago Press.

Simmel, G. (1994/1909) Bridge and door. *Theory Culture, Society*, 11, 5–10.

Simmel, G. (1997) The sociology of space. In D. Frisby and M. Featherstone (eds), *Simmel on culture: Selected writings* (pp. 137–170). London: Sage.

Simmel, G. (1997a) Die probleme der geschichtsphilosophie. *Georg Simmel Gesamtausgabe*, vol. 9. Frankfurt am Main: Suhrkamp.

Simmel, G. (1997b) The metropolis and mental life. In N. Leach (ed.), *Rethinking architecture: A reader in cultural theory* (pp. 69–79). London: Routledge.

Simmel, G. (1999) Lebensanschauung. *Georg Simmel Gesamtausgabe*, vol. 16. Frankfurt am Main: Suhrkamp.

Simmel, G. (2007) The social boundary, translated by Ulrich Teucher and Thomas M. Kemple. *Theory, Culture & Society*, 24(7–8), 53–56.

Simmel, G. (2010/1918) Life as transcendence. In John A. Y. Andrews and Donald N. Levine (trans.), *The view of life: four metaphysical essays, with journal aphorisms*. Chicago: The University of Chicago Press.

Siu, P. (1952) The sojourner. *American Journal of Sociology*, 58(1), 34–44.

Stonequist, E. (1935) The problem of the marginal man. *American Journal of Sociology*, 41(1), 1–12.

Wood, W. (2017) Habit in personality and social psychology. *Personality and Social Psychology Review*, 21(4), 389–403.

2

THE SUBURBS AND THE WORLD

Norbert Elias on incorporation of the stranger

Norbert Elias did not address the issue of the stranger directly or in any detail. However, in this chapter the argument will be developed that it is possible to construct a coherent picture of the stranger by drawing upon Eliasian categories and perspectives. Elias's figurational sociology is based upon a theoretical framework that traces the socio-economic development of the Western European societies from the late medieval period (thirteenth century) up until the modern era. The balance of involvement and detachment is at the centre of Elias's figurational approach to social analysis. Elias identified several broad historical movements such as the processes of state formation, the state's monopoly of legitimate violence, regulation and the more specialised division of labour, by which individuals became more directly and indirectly dependent upon each other. The task of Elias's figurational sociology is to explain how the actions of individuals come to be interdependent, to be bonded to one another in time and space, to interweave their actions to form structures and processes of regulation, mutual control and dependence that cannot be understood as a product of the biological or psychological qualities or features of the individuals themselves. These broad historical movements changed our social structures (sociogenesis) and our personality structures (psychogenesis). Elias is interested in the psychogenesis of individuals within the context of a broader sociogenesis. One of his central arguments is that sociogenesis and psychogenesis are linked and consequently people have developed a more consistently regulated sense of self and a greater sense of social interdependency; which Elias terms the figuration. These changes in the individual psyche are reflected in our attitudes to violence, greater desire for self-restraint, control of the body in public places and manners, and lead directly to the creation of the stranger. The stranger is a person who is outside of the 'civilising process', not bonded, segmented, outside of incorporation and the acceptance of forms of civilised conduct.

There are several interconnected assumptions underpinning Elias's approach to social analysis:

- The human self contains an *I-self* and a *We-self*; humans are dependent on others and for this reason Elias regards the idea of a totally independent individual as unsound: 'Descartes gave the signal: "Cogito ergo sum." What could be more absurd! Merely in order to say it, one had to learn a communal language' (Elias 2007/1987: 14).
- Elias rejects what he refers to as 'ontological dualism'; the notion that the world can be divided into subjects and objects. Subjects cannot exist without objects, even the individual human agent can conceptually step back from self and view themselves as an object. Ontologically we are in a relationship of functional interdependence.
- Although social life is constituted by the intentional actions of human beings who interact with each other, the outcome of human actions coming together is often unplanned and unintended. The role of the sociologists is to identify and explain the mechanics of this transition of intentional human action into unplanned and unintentional patterns of social life. As suggested above, this process of social transformation is described by Elias as 'sociogenesis' and it is linked to the processes of individual psychological development that Elias refers to as 'psychogenesis'.
- Social life is understood in terms of relations or networks of social relations that Elias initially described as 'configurations' or in his later work as 'figurations' – the interrelation or interconnection of

individuals in relationships of dependency. Power for Elias is also a relational and processual concept and 'power ratios' or the distribution of power within any social formation is never static or intrinsically stable but may fluctuate over time.

The Society of Individuals

The Society of Individuals (Elias 2010) is about coming to an understanding of the relationship between the individual and society. In the preface to *The Society of Individuals*, Elias explains that the individual and society are often assumed to be 'two ontologically different entities'; with the term 'society' often falsely understood as an 'unstructured collection of individuals' or equally falsely as an 'object existing beyond individuals' and the individual understood as an 'entity existing in complete isolation' (Elias 2010: 3). The single individual does operate psychologically independently of others in society. All people have an *I-identity* and a *We-identity* and the balance between the two reflects the balance between the individual and society. All individuals are connected by relationships of dependency and interdependency. This framework of human association is a highly segregated operational web of 'interdependent functions, the structure and pattern of which gives society its specific character, is not a creation of particular individuals" (Elias 2010: 19). The web links people both directly and indirectly to form chains of actions that bind people: 'it is this network of the functions which people have for each other, it and nothing else, that we call "society"' (Elias 2010: 20).

Elias draws the analogy with the construction of a house; the relationship between the stones is what forms the complex structure of the house not the shape of the stones themselves. Reason and feelings are not given by nature, they are a product of constraints constructed by people. The way we choose to construct our character as an individual and the self-restraint that we feel internally is something that we can only experience by reference to the 'relational functions' and expectations of others with whom we are associated: 'one must start from the structure of the relations between individuals in order to understand the "psyche" of the individual person' (Elias 2010: 39). The direction of the chains of actions that bind people has a: 'regularity and a tempo of change that are in their turn mightier than the will and plans of a single person within it' (Elias 2010: 47). Power is experienced by the individual as the limits to the scope for action within a given context.

Although power may appear to be suspect and something that people should fear, as it can be used by people to exploit others for their own ends, for Elias power is neither 'good' nor 'bad'; it is a feature or structural characteristic underpinning dependency on others. All humans are interdependent on each other and therefore all of us are potentially vulnerable: 'Power is not an amulet possessed by one person and not by another; it is a structural characteristic of all human relationships – of all human relationships' (Elias 2002/1978: 70).

As chains of dependency become longer and more people become dependent on others, individuals find it difficult to perceive let alone control the web of dependence. As such, the processes of interweaving become: 'relatively self-regulating, and relatively autonomous in relation to the people who form the web of interdependences' (Elias 2002/1978: 91). The individual person can only be understood by their relationship to others. The individual is bound to others through interdependence: 'The structure and configuration of an individual's behaviour-control depend on the structure of the relationship between individuals' (Elias 2010: 59). Relations between people have a regularity or structure that cannot be understood by reference to the individual alone. However, the individual is more than a passive machine. The form of the regularity or structure of the form reflects the experiences of individuals and is shaped by what people wish for (Elias 2010: 79). The 'wished for' form reflects the repetition of experiences, or habits, that underpin what Elias refers to as a social habitus. Practice links the inner world of subjectivity to the outer world of regulation or social habitus. Moreover, it is practice that connects individual thought and social action in the process of transition from individual habit to social habitus (Elias 2010: 115). There is a balance between the *I-Identity*, our personal definition of self, and the *We-Identity*, our identity as part of a group with shared ideas and values; and self-regulation, underpinned by 'conscience' emerges with structural transformation of social life to form the *I–We balance* (Elias 2010: 128): Human beings are 'social beings' and 'the structure of a single person is related to other people and to group life' (Elias 2010: 154).

The social habitus is reflected in the social character or social personality of the individuals within a given figuration. The we-less person is cast as the stranger. For Elias, the we-less person is reflected in the central character of Camus's *The Stranger*:

> One of the peculiarities of the lonely man is that the hero of this book appears to be a curious confusion of the emotions. He kills someone, but the corresponding feelings, whether of hate or remorse, are lacking. His mother dies, but he feels, actually nothing. The feelings of grief or being left behind alone do not arise. Isolation, abandonment are the permanent underlying feelings. They are not associated with people. The I is alone, without any real relation to other people, without the feelings that make the we-relationship possible.
>
> *(Elias 2010: 179)*

The stranger is devoid of 'emotive affirmation' and does not feel the need the need to give or receive the emotional connection from others in a we-relationship. There is a form of exclusion from the habitus imposed on individuals who are unwilling or unable give spontaneous support to others in the we-group who are likely to be perceived as strange; individuals who are unwilling to accept affective relationships we/us. Consequently, because the stranger does not recognise or act upon the shared social habitus they appear to act without regulation or to be without conscience and becomes perceived as the third; a person excluded from the we-identity (Elias 2010: 185).

Difference potentially brings the stranger into conflict with the we-group. There are strong constraints of the habitus that underpin the we-relationship. To be unincorporated is to be able to resist powerful integrative processes and as such the unincorporated appear to the 'we'-group as irrational or unreasonable. People who are not incorporated may have other cultural traditions or cultural memories that they integrated into their identity; traditions or memories that 'we' have never accessed, we have forgotten, we no longer view as significant or that we no longer value. The stranger may 'identify with something beyond the state borders' (Elias 2010: 207). In an appendix to *The Society of Individuals* (2010), which the editors entitled 'Migration and the

Conflict of Generations', Elias identifies migrants as much more likely to be identified as strangers. In the case of migrants, the habitus creates a distance between people that causes recurrent individual problems. The migrant may have traditions, language and morals from their home countries built into their personality structures.

People relate to each other in terms of social and emotional 'involvement' and 'detachment' rather than only in terms of social harmony. The transition is a product of practice rooted in habituation and consequent on the formation of a social habitus by individual people behaving in a regular and predictable manner in a given circumstance. Practice for Elias provides the link between habitual internalisation and incorporation within the social order. Social life is then shaped by habits that form typical ways of behaving that people feel they must be seen to conform to.

In their note on the text of Elias's (2005/1989) *Studies on the Germans*, Stephen Mennell and Eric Dunning explain that in the typescript of the essay, 'The Breakdown of Civilization' Elias chose to use the phrase 'belief and behaviour tradition' as an alternative to the word habitus. 'Belief and behaviour tradition' links personal or individual character with national character; however many people feel uncomfortable using the term 'national character' or 'national pride', however both are components of the 'we-identity' that interconnects individuals within a figuration: 'the question is not whether one thinks national pride is a good or a bad thing. The fact is that it exists' (Elias 2005/1989: 21).

The habitus is reflected in the national language, customs and traditions but is not biologically given and changes over time in conjunction with the processes of state formation:

> a national pattern of behaviour and a closely connected we-image, deeply anchored in the individual personality structure, which represents at the same time both an integral element of the identity of each person, a reliable symbol of a person's belongingness to a group and also the common identity of its members.
>
> *(Elias 2005/1989: 386)*

National pride for Elias is: 'The emotional reward which the individual received from his or her share in the collective value of the nation' (Elias 2005/1989: 388).

For Elias (2005/1989: 385) the we-image is central to the personality structure of the individual and the construction of a person's sense of self-esteem. People who are seen to not share the national character and who do not share the national pride can be perceived as having an 'anti-civilising' character and seen as posing a threat to 'we'. In addition, with specific reference to Germany during the Second World War, Elias argues that 'national idealism' can give people's activities both meaning and a sense of direction. Patriotism and nationalism can give an individual a sense that they are acting in a way that is 'morally good' (Elias 2005/1989: 291). Elias continues by developing an argument that has much in common with Bauman's conception of adiaphoria:

> Particularly in times of national emergency and war, many Germans cheerfully shed the burden of having to control themselves and of having to take responsibility for their own lives. In such situations the state authorities and particularly the symbolic figure at the head of the state, partly or wholly took the place of the individual's own conscience, which thus at the same time established submission to and reverence for the head of state.
>
> *(Elias 2005/1989: 309)*

The coming together of the we-image as central to an individual's construction of self together with the abdication of personal responsibility and its transfer to a person in authority can allow a person to be hostile and engage in acts of violence and cruelty towards the stranger who will be seen as not part of the 'we-identity' and not sharing in our sense of national pride.

> It is simple enough: plans and actions, the emotional and rational impulses of individual people, constantly interweave in a friendly or hostile way. This basic tissue resulting from many single plans and actions of men can give rise to changes and patterns that no individual person has planned or created. From this interdependence of people arises an order sui generis, an order more compelling and stronger than the will and reason of the individual people composing it. It is this order of interweaving human

impulses and strivings, this social order, which determines the
course of historical change; it underlies the civilizing process.

(Elias 1998: 50)

The civilising process sets limits to behaviour and encourages people
to think about the distinction between self and Other in terms of the
degree of self-constraint individuals are capable of exercising. This distinction between self and Other is understood by reference to what
Elias terms *civilite*, which becomes a barrier and a rationale for detachment or exclusion:

> This make-up, the social habitus of individuals forms, as it were,
> the soil from which grow the personal characteristics through
> which an individual differs from other members of his society. In
> this way something grows out of the common language which the
> individual shares with others and which is certainly a component of
> his social habitus – a more or less individual style, what might be
> called an unmistakable individual handwriting that grows out of
> the social script.
>
> *(Elias 2010: 182)*

On the process of civilisation

In the civilising process, differences between the emerging affluent
middle class and the courtly upper class were reflected in differences in
behaviour, emotional life and morality:

> courtly people wished to designate, in a broad or narrow sense, the
> specific quality of their own behaviour, and by which they con-
> trasted the refinement of their own social manners, their 'standard'
> with the manners of simpler and socially inferior people.
>
> *(Elias 2012/1939: 47)*

The European upper class drew upon a concept of *homme civilise* as a
form of social criticism to define themselves as distinct and separate
from others who were less civilised. Court society was a new form of
social formation that emerged with a distinct changes and disruption in

the figuration. The concept of *civilite* developed in Western society at a time when the Catholic Church was losing some of its influence in public life and 'knightly society' was also in decline. Elias outlines the influence of Erasmus of Rotterdam's influential 1530 treatise on manners *De civilitate morum puerilium* (On the civility of boys). Manners reflected the character of the person. Cultured people developed a consciousness of their own superiority. The use of manners became a vehicle to express a preferred class-based self-image and people attempted to define themselves as more cultured and civilised than people in lower class positions. Cultural institutions, such as schools and legal institutions, were used for self-improvement as well as the advancement of knowledge.

In Elias's view, two ideas can be identified within the French concept of *civilisation* and the German conception of *Kultur*; first by defining oneself as civilised as opposed to people who behaved in a barbaric manner. Good manners, it was assumed, reflected the 'higher gifts' of the person who exhibited them; good manners were also to be seen to act in conformity with socially good behaviour and to exhibit ways of behaving that were appropriate and acceptable within court society circles. Good manners reflected one's social position as legitimate. Habits, rules and taboos may change over time and reflect the changing nature of manners; however, the direction of change was towards greater internal pacification, and manners exercised a social control function. People were expected to conform and adapt their behaviour. To be seen to deviate from the acceptable ways of behaving was to place oneself outside of the figuration and to become an outsider. Not surprisingly, Elias explained:

'The stranger to the country has a particularly difficult time' (Elias 2012/1939: 80).

Elias explains that there is nothing 'natural' about the adoption of table manners such as choosing to eat with a fork, choosing not to spit or blow one's nose at the table, and the negative emotions and sense of revulsion or the feeling of embarrassment associated when observing others doing these things. The adoption of table manners, and of civil behaviour in general, is about the way in which behaviours are moulded:

> the change in behaviour at table was part of a much larger trans-
> formation of human feelings and attitudes. It also illuminates the
> degree to which the motors of this development came from the

social structure, from the way in which people were related to or
integrated with each other.

(Elias 2012/1939: 117)

The displeasure we feel in relation to the way people choose to conduct themselves at the table is a product of practice. The practice of good
manners: 'arises through habit … an inner automatism, the imprint of
society on the inner self, the super ego' (Elias 2012/1939: 128). Ways of
behaving become 'second nature', as people come to exercise self-
restraint even when they are alone: 'The feeling of shame was clearly a
social function moulded according to the social structure' (Elias 2012/
1939: 137). Habits are personal but socially patterned.

The civilising process also applied to the regulation of people's
sexuality. Sexual activity became increasingly regulated and legitimate
sexual activity was seen to be only between a man and a woman. In
addition, acting upon sexual impulses became progressively more pri-
vatised with conducting sexual activities in public becoming strictly
prohibited. The nuclear family became a legitimate place to exercise
one's sex activities and the institution that regulated and controlled the
sexual impulses of young people. The behaviours and habits of parents
are passed on to their children and form part of the child's character.
Elias uses the word *intimisation* to describe the growth of privacy in
relation to sexuality. However: 'The process of civilisation does not
follow a straight line' (Elias 2012/1939: 181) as tensions in relation to
the balance of power within figurations can impact on the dynamics,
pace and direction of civilisation. However, the complete '*intimisation*'
of all bodily functions underpinned the civilising process. The Freudian
conception of 'superego' is used by Elias to identify the: 'correspon-
dence between the social structure and the structure of the personality,
of the individual self' (Elias 2012: 185). The division of labour was a
key factor in the civilising process. Specialisation of work techniques
was needed to satisfy the increasingly complex products and services
that people wanted to consume. This specialisation made individuals
increasingly dependent upon each other within a money economy.

In earlier phases of history, the ownership and control of economic
power also meant having military power and jurisdiction: 'Without
violent actions, without the motive forces of free competition, there

would be no monopoly of force, and thus no pacification, no suppression and control of violence over larger areas' (Elias 2012/1939: 346). Elias identifies two phases in the development of monopolies: the stage of free competition leading to the formation of private monopolies and the gradual conversion of the private into the public monopoly. With the increasing commercialisation and use of a single currency, bourgeois groups demanded protection from physical violence to allow greater opportunities to make money and distribute goods within larger geographical areas. The 'royal mechanism', a centralised strong state, emerged to facilitate commerce and reduce conflict.

Although individuals may desire more possessions, the human web has a tendency towards the formation of monopoly state rule, but within the figuration people oppose the private monopolisation of state resources such as revenue from taxation. At the same time the shift in power towards a centralised state meant there was a greater legal obligation on people to pay taxes. The process of civilisation occurred in a largely unplanned fashion, but neither was it a product of random actions, nature, or a reflection of the uniformities or orderliness of the mind:

> This continuous, interweaving of people's separate plans and actions, can give rise to changes and patterns that no individual person has planned or created. From this interdependence of people arises an order sui generis, an order more compelling and stronger than the will and reason of the individual people composing it.
>
> *(Elias 2012/1939: 404)*

The result is that pressure is brought to bear on individuals to act on their own reflections and develop an 'agency of control' over libidinal impulses, which becomes part of the personality structure of the individual (Elias 2012/1939: 411–412). Elias refers to this 'agency of control', which becomes part of the personality structure of the individual, as the 'superego' agency that is formed by the 'habituation to affect-inhibition' (Elias 2012/1939: 414). Pacification is then the reduction of disruptive conflicts and behavioural irregularities by self-regulation and the internalised control of libidinal impulses within the social field.

Elias on Jews in history

Elias's work has been largely ignored in the study of Jewish history. In the Middle Ages, strangers, above all Jews, were held responsible for the plague and large numbers of them were massacred in the twentieth century by the National Socialists who also used similar 'fantasy-laden' explanations for collective miseries by again identifying the actions of Jews and other relatively powerless minorities as the cause (Elias 2002/1978: 21–22). The Jew is often presented as the stranger and Elias's work could be used to very good effect to explain the processes of estrangement experienced by many Jewish people throughout European history. In his foreword to Steven Russell's (1996) book on the connection between Jewish identity and Elias's conception of the civilising processes, Stephen Mennell (1996) explains that Russell's argument demonstrates how the European Jews had a significant role to play in the long-term processes of structural change. This role was not only in relation to business but also as 'Court Jews', a role that Russell sees as central to the processes of state formation. However, Jews remained as an outsider group in relation to the more accepted Christian groups:

> Beside a traditional sense of community with its strongest support in the common faith and its most important promoters in the clergy – but which never prevents disintegration, nor of itself brings about an alliance, merely strengthening and guiding it in certain directions – the urge to conquer and the necessity of resisting conquest is the most fundamental factor binding together people in regions lying relatively far apart.
>
> *(Elias 1939: 29, cited in Mennell 1996: 3–4)*

The very slow and uneven pace of Jewish emancipation is regarded by Russell as one of the most controversial and difficult to understand aspects of the Jewish experience in Europe since the Middle Ages. In the early medieval period religion was still the dominant factor in the processes of social formation and the processes of exclusion and estrangement.

A central aspect of Elias's work is the administration of increasingly large and widely spread territories and consequent growth and development of state 'administrative apparatuses'. Educated Jewish people had a role to play in the new bureaucratic and administrative structures. Russell notes that anti-Jewish feeling at this time was often related to their unique legal status of Jewish people and their influence in public affairs; as we saw above, what Elias calls the 'royal mechanism'. For a shrewd sovereign, Jewish people could be used to balance opposing forces and influence power ratios in favour of the sovereign. Jewish funds and influence could be used by the sovereign power to keep in check disruptive forces:

> Put in more explicitly Eliasian terms: largely as a result of the unique situations they occupied in the constantly changing power figurations, they were particularly useful to central rulers in both inter- and intra-figurational transactions. This usefulness was undoubtedly hazardous for the Jews.
>
> *(Russell 1996: 34)*

Russell reports on how Oliver Cromwell's republic was financially strained because of the cost of revolution and war and drew upon financial resources provided by financiers such as Samson Wertheimer of Vienna (1658–1728), who was able to 'assemble packages of loans raised, with the help of fellow Jews, in a dozen different places at once' (Israel 1985: 132 cited in Russell 1996: 31).

However, despite influence in public affairs across Europe the legal status of the Jews was generally unclear and often ambiguous. Many people were angry about the ways in which Jews were assumed to be responsible for increasing the level of indebtedness in the population and calls for the confiscation of Jewish property and cancelation of debts was common. In Eliasian terms, Jewish people could often find themselves in the conflict brought about by shifting influence with fluctuating power figurations.

Involvement and detachment

Self-distancing and detachment are about the creation of 'social compartments' (what Elias was to later refer to as 'ordered segmentation') within which to place others (Elias 2007/1987: 35) in order to describe other people as 'we', 'you' or 'them'. Groups generate a 'we image' in contrast to a 'they image', with people who are assigned a 'they image' also being understood to have a 'they' perspective. One element that helps to shape the level of involvement and detachment is the perception of danger and the fear that this can generate. In the past, non-human agents such as natural forces were regarded as a source of fear and danger. The greater control over nature has given people a greater sense of security. However, people have come to feel secure, argues Elias, but even minor forms of tension or friction can bring about 'not knowing' and generate fear. For Elias the same processes that have made people less dependent on nature have made people more dependent upon each other. If the Other is regarded as uncontrollable, this can generate fear.

Not knowing is a condition that human agents do not like as it generates uncertainty. Human agents within groups engage in the transmission of knowledge to others within the group in order to generate knowledge about what was previously not known. Involvement and detachment are tools for thinking in relation to how to appropriately categorise some thing or somebody. Involvement and detachment are rooted in practice in that our engagement with either involvement or detachment is based upon the guidance we draw upon from the values and beliefs of the we-group. The range of variation in terms of the degree of application of involvement and detachment and our emotional response is limited by: 'the public standards embodied in modes of thinking and speaking' (Elias 2007/1987: 70).

There is for Elias an: 'interdependence between the structure of society at large and the personality structure of individuals, between what are often distinguished as macro- and micro-structure' (Elias 2007/1987: 64). People are 'inescapably chained to each other' (Elias 2007/1987: 78).

Figurations have a process-character for Elias as they are in a constant state of flux. Practice is drawn upon by the human agents to navigate the state of fluidity and fluctuation within the figuration. Functional interdependence provides emotional balance in that interdependence acts as a 'protective shell'. The underpinning guidance provided by the stock of knowledge about a person and how we should categorise them shapes our appropriate attitude towards them. Thinking is described by Elias as 'the silent manipulation of social symbols' (Elias 2007/1987:

118), an interaction between the social fund of knowledge and our own perception and judgement. Access to the social stock of knowledge protects the individual from 'innocent self-centredness' and enhances our individual capacity for identifying potential dangers and the insecurity of not knowing: 'All planned social practices take place within a stream of unplanned and aimless, through structured, processes at a variety of interdependent levels' (Elias 2007/1987: 115).

Societies are viewed by Elias as networks of functionally interdependent human beings who are bound together in figurations. The structures that people create have far reaching consequences for the individuals who form them. Mutual economic cooperation and the benefits of trade are directly related to the state's legitimate use of physical force. Human civilisation requires a high degree of predictable self-constraint and internal pacification that is reinforced by external agencies that have the right to use violence to maintain peaceful coexistence within society. The state monopoly of legitimate physical force allows for economic cooperation as it is used to manage trust in economic exchange and discourage people from engaging in theft rather than trade: 'human groups bound to each other without a central monopoly of physical violence inevitably live in a continuous state of insecurity' (Elias 2007/1987: 144).

The processes of estrangement for Elias are a product of placing a given individual, about which there is a great deal that is unknown and whose co-presence gives us a feeling of insecurity, within a category that we deem appropriate based upon our grasp of the stock of knowledge within a figuration. Practice and cognition are 'of a piece' (Elias 2007/1987: 164). However, 'voluntarist' accounts of the formation of functional interdependence are described by Elias as 'insufficient' as although people 'act wilfully' with the framework of functional interdependence the framework itself is 'not wilfully produced' (Elias 2007/1987: 149).

Established–outsider figuration

According to Stephen Mennell, Elias's theory of established–outsider relations has been 'overshadowed by his theory of the civilizing process' (Mennell 1992: 137).

The Established and the Outsiders (Elias and Scotson 2008/1965) is Elias's account of how members of a group maintain amongst themselves the belief that they are better human beings than others. The research is a case study of a place that Elias and Scotson called Winston Parva, a largely working-class suburban ethnically white community near Leicester. The community was divided into three zones; with a distinct and well-defined division. Zone 1, known by the residents as 'the Village', contained a well-established group who had been resident for several generations and had a coherent community culture and ingroup favouritism, that Elias and Scotson (2008/1965) describe as containing a 'distinguishing group charisma' attributed to itself. The group charisma allowed the group to think of themselves as better than the residents of the other two zones in human terms. The people in zones 2 and 3 were regarded as 'newcomers', 'less well bred' and people who did not belong. Zone 3 was described by the Villagers as the Estate. Unlike the Villagers, who had well-established roots, many of the newcomers became resident in the area because they had had to move to work in a local factory that had an important role to play in the war effort. They came from different parts of the country and were not known to each other before their arrival. This made it difficult for the newcomers to establish a community life of their own. Elias's understanding of the 'established–outsider' relations is important in understanding the position of the stranger. Strangers are outsiders, they are not regarded as part of the 'established' group; as such, they are relatively powerless when compared with the established insider. Elias's work addresses several central sociological questions in relation to social change and stability. The feeling of group superiority provides members of that group with 'an immense narcissistic gratification', a 'gratification of their self-esteem'. The values and beliefs of the we-group are described by Elias as 'a remarkable blend of self-love and altruism, of narcissistic gratification and devotion to a collective' (Elias 2007/1987: 9).

Winston Parva is a case study for 'established' and 'outsider' social relations and the mechanisms of power and stigma, which Elias believed could be found in many other social contexts. There is also a link between Elias's conception of the established–outsider figuration and his theory of the civilising process. Labelling the outsiders with negative characteristics is one of the mechanisms used by the established to establish and reinforce a stigma onto the outsiders. At the same time the successful application of a negative label helps to reinforce the positive self-evaluation of the established. The established always attempt to present themselves as more 'civilised' than the outsiders. In the case of Winston Parva, the people from the Estate were much more likely to be labelled as 'rough' rather than 'respectable' or 'decent'.

Elias's argument suggests that people have developed a greater capacity for empathy and this is reflected in a long-term decline in inter-individual violence in Western society, and a growing sensitisation to violence because of the development of internal and external controls in relation to aggressive behaviour. Consequently, those who do not adapt to the intricacies of social conduct, for example by being aggressive or behaving in a non-restrained manner, come to be seen as acting in an 'uncivilised' manner; similarly, to appear to be not in control of one's emotions is also seen as being 'uncivilised'. To experience such a lack of physical or emotional control would for most people generate a sense of shame.

The residents of the Village kept a distinct and well-defined division between themselves and the residents of the other two zones, maintained by the force of local tradition. Insiders maintained their preferred identity with a combination of exclusion and stigmatisation. The image of the residents in zone 3 was affected by the activities of a small minority of 'problem families', whose reputation was maintained by gossip passed between people of the village as news. In contrast, the reputation of zone 1 was improved by a scattering of 'socially better' families. The Village residents took up the struggle against what they saw as 'the intruders' by closing their ranks against the newcomers:

> They cold-shouldered them. They excluded them from all posts of social power whether in local politics, in voluntary associations or in any other local organisation where their own influence dominated. Above all, they developed as weapons an 'ideology', a system of attitudes and beliefs which stressed and justified their own superiority and which stamped the people on the Estate as people of an inferior kind.
>
> *(Elias and Scotson 2008/1965: 59)*

The older residents of the Village still spoke of people from the Estate as 'foreigners', saying that they 'couldn't understand a word they say' (Elias and Scotson 2008/1965: 59).

According to Elias and Scotson, these dynamics of exclusion are an inherent part of an established outsider-figuration. The exclusion of one or more groups from all power resources can help to establish 'cultural', educational and emotional differences within any community. There is a close connection between 'power' and 'self-esteem', according to Elias and Scotson. In any established-outsider figuration there is always an unequal distribution of power, status and resources. 'Having power' is understood as being worth more and loss of power is perceived as loss of worth. This 'logic of emotions' is, according to Elias and Scotson, the reason why established groups attempt to stigmatise outsiders. Perhaps surprisingly most of the residents of the Estate, albeit grudgingly, accepted the lower status given to them by the Villagers and accepted that their community had a bad reputation.

The theoretical framework Elias and Scotson developed was based upon the assumption that it was methodologically unsound to make a division between agency and structure:

> The conceptual and methodological separation of enquiries into the structure of human groupings at a given time and enquiries into the structure of the processes in the course of which they became what they were, showed itself, in the case, to be wholly artificial.
>
> *(Elias and Scotson 2008/1965: 62)*

For Elias, interdependencies of configuration or what was to later become 'figurations' of human beings are essential to understanding social life. Exclusion and stigmatisation are not forms of prejudice rooted in the personality of the individual, rather exclusion takes the form of detachment, distancing and stigmatisation by which the other is regarded as contaminating. This opinion becomes a collective fantasy or 'village spirit', which is central to the formation and maintenance of a figuration. Elias uses the term *nomie* to describe the 'village spirit' and the role of the village spirit is to provide social coherence and a shared understanding of the norm. The figuration is used by Elias as a conceptual device to explain how group opinion and individual self-control are interconnected with each other:

> Nothing in the observable evidence corresponds to a con-ceptualisation such as 'individual' and 'society', which implies that there are, in fact, individuals without society and societies without individuals which form in some way separate groups of objects and can be studied separately without reference to each other ... Indi-viduals always come in configurations and configurations of indivi-duals are irreducible. To start thinking from a single individual as if it were initially independent of all others or from single individuals here and there irrespective of their relationships to each other is a fictitious point of departure ... [configuration means] a plurality of individuals who in one or the other way are interdependent.
>
> *(Elias and Scotson 2008/1965: 192–193)*

For Elias the figuration: 'can have a compelling power over the indi-viduals which form them' (Elias and Scotson 2008/1965: 195).

The stranger for Elias is an outsider within established–outsider fig-uration. Elias argues that insider–outsider relations have common ele-ments in all cultures. The stranger as outsider is seen as inferior, is often described as an animal and a person whose presence violates the 'good order': 'the outsider group may be credited with an offensive smell; bodily nearness may be experienced as disagreeable; bodily touch (however accidental) as blemish and dirtying' (Elias 1990: 228–229). Elias gives the examples of Jews in Nazi Germany and Black Americans in the Southern States of America in the 1950s. Outsider groups are excluded from chances of exercising power or status and from access to information. As Russell observes: 'Less "civilized" behaviour will be increasingly likely to carry considerable costs in terms of the diminution of power chances and of one's place in a social figuration' (Russell 1996: 16). However, for Elias, people relate to each other, when they are in conflict as well as when they seek co-operation.

Elias's argument on conflict and co-operation underpinning inter-dependencies predates Judith Butler's understanding of the relation between the self and the Other at the heart of identities, which she derives from her reading of Hegel's lord and bondsman relation.

Recognition is a constant theme in Elias's social analysis and his argument has much in common with Judith Butler's understanding of recognition. In *Subjects of Desire: Hegelian Reflections in Twentieth-Century France*, Butler (1987) takes her starting point from Hegel's *Phenomenology of Spirit* in which he looks at the concept of desire and the link between subjectivity and alterity in what has become known as the Lord–Bondsman scenario. For Hegel, desire and self-consciousness emerge side by side, and self-consciousness is rooted in desire in general. For Butler, Hegel's concept of desire is a general, essential characteristic of human consciousness and a central feature of our subjectivity: 'if this unity is to take place, and one of the terms of this unity is the sensuous world, then it makes sense to assume that self-consciousness itself must have a sensuous expression' (Butler 1987: 33).

Butler reads Hegel's phenomenology not as a philosophical truth but as a series of 'instructive fictions' in which the relation between subjectivity and desire is plotted. This is reflected in the struggle for recognition between Lord and Bondsman. On Butler's reading of Hegel's *Phenomenology of Spirit*, Hegel explains how an individual subject must suffer his own loss of identity again and again in order to achieve his greatest sense of self – and become an 'ek-static' or decentred subject, in which the self is dependent on something outside itself.

The Lord–Bondsman situation presents what Butler sees as the idea of intersubjective recognition. Self-consciousness attempts to secure confirmation of itself through the 'negation' – the consumption of material objects. However, the problem with attempting to satisfy desire by consumption is that it requires a 'constant activity of negation' (Butler 1987: 39). When we consume we destroy the object. Self-consciousness comes to realise that it needs a being like itself – another self-consciousness (or other) so that it can affirm itself as an autonomous being. However, self-consciousness comes to realise that in its desire to be confirmed by the other it becomes dependent on the other. The subject attempts to assert its supremacy by 'negating' the other and the other attempts to preserve its own autonomy by resisting. The winner does not destroy the other but enslaves the other; two equal co-present self-consciousnesses come together as a consciousness that is independent (Lord) and a consciousness that is dependent (Bondsman) whose desire is to live for or be for the other. In a similar fashion, it is also the case in Elias's work that it is through this self-loss, recognition and cultivation of relations of dependence that people become sustainable social beings within figurations.

According to Quilley and Loyal (2004), in explaining his contribution to social analysis, Elias emphasised two key concepts – *hominess aperti* and reality-congruent knowledge. *Hominess aperti* is concerned with the 'people' rather than the individual person; the processes and movements of people across generations and understanding social life within the context of interdependencies. Elias's reality-congruent approaches embrace strategies by which the researcher's attempts to suspend moral and political convictions diminish the influence of their values on their research.

Taking their starting point from Norbert Elias on the civilising process, Hélène Joffe and Christian Staerklé argue that: 'Individualism is a core value in western culture, and one of its key components, self-control, has become an organizing principle of personhood' (Joffe and Staerklé 2007: 396). Self-control, as reflected in self-discipline, perseverance, self-denial and will-power has become a 'master value' in societies in which an individualist ideology is promoted. Such forms of self-control, or the ability to actively control desires, emotions and actions, have become to be seen as desirable attributes associated with socially valued and successful individuals: 'Controlling one's body equates to upholding a moral duty to tame the "natural" and disorderly state of the body' (Joffe and Staerklé 2007: 407). These range from 'instinctive' or 'natural' urges in relation to sexuality, hunger-based control, and control over bodily fluids, to resisting addictions, for example smoking. People who are identified as belonging to an outgroup are assumed to have little self-control in all aspects of their lives, and for this reason Joffe and Staerklé suggest that self-control has become an 'instrument of exclusion and derogation' (Joffe and Staerklé 2007: 396).

Joffe and Staerklé survey the research in the field to suggest that people lacking in self-control are likely to become labelled as uncivilised strangers; such groups can include individuals from non-Western cultural contexts (Said 1978; Sanchez-Mazas 2004; Staerklé 2005); some women (Glick and Fiske 1996; Lorenzi-Cioldi 1998), children (Chombart de Lauwe 1984); the mentally ill (Jodelet 1991); the association of gay men with promiscuity (Herek 1998), obese people with weakness of will-power (Crandall 1994), drug users and smokers with connotations of addiction (Echebarria Echabe, Fernandez Guede, and Gonzalez Castro 1994), and poor people lacking self-sufficiency and control over destiny (Feather 1999; Gilens 1999).

The negative personal traits are applied to people within these social categories. The social categories are neither neutral nor arbitrary but are generated by the way in which a socially meaningful comparison is internalised by individuals as part of their taken-for-granted assumptions. Such social categories become part of the shared understanding within a group and provide the foundation for making social exclusion feel legitimate.

As suggested by the underpinning assumptions within practice theory, and drawing upon Billig (2002), Joffe and Staerklé (2007) accept that: 'individuals do not create their own categories but assimilate the categories that are culturally available, thereby accepting culturally determined patterns of prejudgement and stereotyping' (Billig 2002: 175). As such, the breaking of norms or standards, such as obesity, unattractiveness or unpleasant body odour, is used to identify individuals and groups and provides the justification for stigmatisation and exclusion. Exclusion has an underpinning intuitive, emotional and symbolic foundation associated with the identification of individuals with dirt, perversity and moral inferiority; qualities all assumed to be rooted in personal failings, such as lack of responsibility and lack of self-control.

Incorporation

Although Elias does not explain in any detail the concept of incorporation in the civilising process it was more fully developed by Eric Dunning and colleagues in their research into crowd disorder at football matches. Dunning and colleagues draw upon Elias's conception of state formation and pacification to explain that the working class became increasingly 'incorporated' over the course of the nineteenth century and became increasingly uncomfortable and appalled at acts of violence in public places. Taking their starting point from Elias, Dunning et al. argue that the social world is a product of the situated activities of human agents. As they explain: 'The social world is constituted by thinking, feeling and acting human beings. It cannot be properly understood independently either of its location in time and space or the processes that occur in that connection' (Dunning, Murphy and Williams 1988: 217).

At the centre of Dunning et al.'s conception of incorporation is a notion of a culturally deprived rough underclass that in the United Kingdom had been popularized by the Thatcher governments in the 1980s. Dunning and colleagues view the working-class individuals who engage in crowd disorder as:

> severely restrained in the formation of their personalities, their values and their actions by their restricted life experiences, their lack of comparative knowledge, and by constraints which lead to their interest and involvement in publicly aggressive forms of masculinity and 'street style'.
>
> *(Dunning et al. 1988: 220)*

Incorporation is the acceptance of forms of civilised conduct. Dunning et al.'s argument focuses on the rough working class forming an 'ordered segmentation', structurally disconnected, free from civilising tendencies, with their own set of 'moral standards' that underpin their rough behaviour. A group who have remained less incorporated. This ordered group have limited opportunities to exercise power compared with all other income groups in the population and this has:

> manifold consequences for their personality, their perception of other groups, their social standards and the structure of the communities they form ... Given the circumstances in which they live, a strict and prohibiting 'conscience' or 'super ego' with regard to engaging in and/or watching fights is liable to be unusual.
>
> *(Dunning et al. 1988: 240)*

Dunning and colleagues argue that 'ordered segmentation' has the effect of confining people into a given milieu, which limits their life chances and life experiences.

Conclusion

From an Elias perspective, the stranger is a category of person who is not incorporated and is subjected to a form of 'ordered segmentation'. Ordered segmentation is the emergence of a separate cultural grouping within a wider community, which remains structurally disconnected from the broad sweep of civilising tendencies. Within the confines of the ordered segmentation people develop their own set of 'moral standards' that emerge from the experience of living within a given locality and these 'moral standards' underpin their behaviour.

An Elias inspired conception of the stranger, however, is not solely composed of rough working-class people, as in Dunning et al.'s conception of incorporation. The stranger is viewed as distinct and separate from the 'we' group. The stranger is an outsider, paced outside of the established-outsider figuration. The Elias conception of stranger is a 'we-less' person, devoid of 'emotive affirmation' and without the need to give and receive affect from 'us' the Established in a we-relationship. The stranger does not recognise or act upon the shared social habitus and appears to act without regulation or to be without conscience.

The Eliasian superego is constructed out of moral judgements about right and wrong that people acquire through the processes of socialisation and integrated into self. Elias is then suggesting that the unincorporated other is the stranger inside us all. The stranger may exhibit ways of behaving that suggest to people brought up with a given figuration that the stranger has a limited 'agency of control' over their libidinal impulses and as such is incapable of affect-inhibition. The stranger has a psycho-social character and is a symbol of the unincorporated and dangerous Other. This representation of the unincorporated and dangerous Other is everything that the superego has led us to believe that we are not. A conception of the stranger from an Eliasian perspective has much in common with Bauman's (1991) concept of the familiar stranger. The stranger is slimy, a character who is polluted and contaminated and whose presence we find threatening. The stranger is a projection of our internalised fear of difference and fear of becoming psychologically invaded by Otherness.

References

Bauman, Z. (1991) *Modernity and ambivalence*. Cambridge: Polity.
Billig, M. (2002) Henri Tajfel's 'Cognitive aspects of prejudice' and the psychology of bigotry. *British Journal of Social Psychology*, 41, 171–188.

Butler, J. (1987) *Subjects of desire: Hegelian reflections in twentieth-century France.* New York: Columbia University Press.

Chombart de Lauwe, M. J. (1984) Changes in the representation of the child in the course of social transmission. In R.W. Farr & S. Moscovici (eds), *Social representations* (pp. 185–209). Cambridge: Cambridge University Press.

Crandall, C. S. (1994) Prejudice against fat people: Ideology and self-interest. *Journal of Personality and Social Psychology*, 66, 882–894.

Dunning, E., Murphy, P. and Williams, J. (1988) *The roots of football hooliganism.* London: Routledge.

Echebarria Echabe, A., Fernandez Guede, E. and Gonzalez Castro, C. (1994) Social representations and intergroup conflicts: Who's smoking here? *European Journal of Social Psychology*, 3, 339–356.

Elias, N. (1990) Further aspects of established–outsider relations: The Maycomb model. In N. Elias and J. L. Scotson (1965, 2008), *The established and the outsiders. The collected works of Norbert Elias vol. 4*, edited by C. Wouters (pp. 209–231). Dublin: University College Dublin Press.

Elias, N. (1998) The social constraint towards self-constraint. In N. Elias and S. Mennell (eds), *On civilization, power, and knowledge: Selected writings* (pp. 49–66). Chicago: University of Chicago Press.

Elias, N. (2002/1978) What is sociology? In A. Bogner, K. Liston and S. Mennell (eds), *The collected works of Norbert Elias vol. 5*, trans. G. Morrissey, S. Mennell and E. Jephcott. Dublin: University College Dublin Press.

Elias, N. (2005/1989) *Studies on the Germans: Power struggles and the development of habitus in the nineteenth and twentieth centuries. Collected works of Norbert Elias vol. 11.* Edited by S. Mennell and E. Dunning. Dublin: University College Dublin Press.

Elias, N. (2007/1987) *Involvement and detachment, the collected works of Norbert Elias vol. 8.* Edited by S. Quilley. Dublin: University College Dublin Press.

Elias, N. (2010) *The society of individuals.* Dublin: University College Dublin Press.

Elias, N. (2012/1939) *On the process of civilisation: Sociogenetic and psychogenetic investigations. The collected works of Norbert Elias vol. 3.* Edited by S. Mennell, E. Dunning and R. Kilminister. Dublin: University College Dublin Press.

Elias, N. and Scotson, J. L. (2008/1965) *The established and the outsiders, the collected works of Norbert Elias vol. 4.* Edited by C. Wouters. Dublin: University College Dublin Press.

Feather, N. (1999) Judgments of deservingness: Studies in the psychology of justice and achievement. *Personality and Social Psychology Review*, 3, 86–107.

Gilens, M. (1999) *Why Americans hate welfare.* Chicago, IL: University of Chicago Press.

Glick, P. and Fiske, S. T. (1996) The ambivalent sexism inventory: Differentiating hostile and benevolent sexism. *Journal of Personality and Social Psychology*, 70, 491–512.

Herek, G. M. (ed.). (1998) *Stigma and sexual orientation: Understanding prejudice against lesbians, gay men, and bisexuals*. Thousand Oaks, CA: Sage.

Jodelet, D. (1991) *Madness and social representations*. Hemel Hempstead: Harvester-Wheatsheaf.

Joffe, H. and Staerklé, C. (2007) The centrality of the self-control ethos in western aspersions regarding outgroups: A social representational approach to stereotype content. *Culture and Psychology*, 13(4), 395–341.

Lorenzi-Cioldi, F. (1998) Group status and perceptions of homogeneity. *European Review of Social Psychology*, 9, 31–75.

Mennell, S. (1992) *Norbert Elias: An introduction*. Oxford: Blackwell.

Mennell, S. (1996) Foreword. In S. Russell, *Jewish identity and civilizing processes*. Basingstoke: Macmillan.

Quilley, S. and Loyal, S. (2004) *The sociology of Norbert Elias*. Cambridge: Cambridge University Press.

Russell, S. (1996) *Jewish identity and civilizing processes*. Basingstoke: Macmillan.

Said, E. W. (1978) *Orientalism: Western conceptions of the orient*. London: Penguin.

Sanchez-Mazas, M. (2004) *Racisme et xénophobie*. Paris: Presses Universitaires de France.

Staerklé, C. (2005) L'idéal démocratique perverti: Représentations antagonistes dans la mise en altérité du non-Occident. In M. Sanchez-Mazas and L. Licata (eds), *L'autre: Regards psychosociaux* (pp. 117–148). Grenoble: Presses Universitaires de Grenoble.

3

THE CAMPS AND THE STRANGER

Bauman

There is no such thing, claims Bauman as an 'inclusive community', for fraternity always requires a stranger. And while being in a swarm is meaningful for the individual, it is only because there is some other individual who has been excluded … The need for security in liquid modernity can be in fact so desperate, comments Bauman, that explosive communities can easily spring up and portray violence and sacrifice as essential means for defending unity and maintaining harmony.

(Oxenham 2013: 31)

Across his writings Zygmunt Bauman always kept coming back to the question: What is the substance of modernity? This chapter attempts to identify if there is a coherent set of characteristics of the stranger across Zygmunt Bauman's conceptions of solid modernity, postmodernity and liquid modernity. The chapter will explore how Bauman defines and identifies the stranger, the experience of strangeness and the conditions he identifies that give rise to the emergence of the stranger within society. Bauman's construction of who is a stranger draws upon many of the ideas, arguments and authors discussed in the previous chapters and as such his understanding of the stranger has shifted with his analysis of modernity. Bauman's stranger is not the same in solid modernity as it was in his sociology of postmodernity or his liquid turn writings. Although overall for Bauman the experience of strangerhood in solid, post and liquid modernity is one of dislocation, infused with 'existential ambivalence', it is the experience of estrangement that generates a life that is endemically precarious and born out of rootlessness. However, Bauman's commentators on the stranger have failed to notice that there are deep contradictions between Bauman's conception of the stranger in solid, post and liquid modernity.

Modernity has experienced a transition from what Bauman (2007) identifies as the 'solid' conception of modernity characterised by a centralised administrative state that exercises power over life with a clearly identified geographical location. Solid modernity is rooted in an obsession and compulsion for order-making. However, 'Some people cannot adapt and do not fit' (Bauman and Tablet 2017: 135). It is these people who are unable to adapt and do not fit who become the strangers. The 'stranger is ambivalence incarnated; it is the tangible, visible, audible representation of the ambivalence of being' (Bauman and Tablet 2017: 139).

Bauman's answer to the question 'Why do people in solid modernity like order?' revolves around Mary Douglas's conceptions of clean and dirty. Bauman suggests that within each person there is an element that is regarded as *slime* or *dirt* that the solid modern person would like to expel from the body. This contaminated, dirty and slimy element is excluded from self and placed into the body and essence of the person who does not belong, the stranger. The solid modern state used the idea of the contaminated Other as a resource to provide stability and counter any and all forms of ambiguity or ambivalence.

In contrast the 'liquid' phase of modernity society has come to be regarded as a fluid 'network' rather than a hard 'structure':

> In my opinion, community has been replaced by networks. Every day you contact many more persons that you do not actually see than persons who you do see. You contact them by email, Twitter or via 'likes' on their 'profile', but you do not feel them physically. You belong to the community, whereas networks belong to you: community considers you as its property, whereas your network hardly notices your existence. On social networks, for example,

you are completely free to kick any network-related individual out at any time, by stopping to use the network or by pressing the 'un-friend' button.

(Bauman and Tablet 2017: 143)

Events in one part of the world can have significant consequences elsewhere: '"Markets without frontiers" is a recipe for injustice' (Bauman 2007: 8). The solid structures that previously limited indivi-dual choices, and the institutions that successfully maintained the rou-tines, patterns of acceptable behaviour are no longer effective in liquid modernity. The liquid modern state can no longer provide insurance to protect its citizens against ill health, unemployment and poverty. In addition, liquid modernity is characterised by a diminishing of com-passion. People who find themselves in poverty are no longer viewed as victims of circumstance and as such the responsibility of the 'commu-nity' but as products of individual failure, ignorance and helplessness. In solid modernity the welfare state or the social state was a communal resource that people could draw upon during times of greatest need. In liquid modernity the welfare state or the social state is viewed as 'our' money and resources given to 'them' – the people who choose to fail. The poor are no longer viewed as a 'reserve army of labour' that should be kept in a decent shape until the economy improves and allows them to return to employment, rather the poor have become a superfluous, supernumerary and redundant, waste population. A 'surplus population' that is unwanted. It is up to individuals to provide themselves with protection in social life by living behind walls, hiring guards to protect their gated communities, driving SUV vehicles that offer greater pro-tection, carrying mace or hand guns and taking martial arts classes.

The processes of liquefaction have brought about a separation of power and politics. In the face of negative global forces, the state no longer has the capacity for long-term planning. Sovereignty is now contested both in terms of meaning and function as the nation state must compete with other bodies on the global stage to exercise sover-eignty. Sovereignty has become 'unanchored and free-floating' (Bauman 2012: 50) and with this comes greater fear and insecurity that people must deal with as part of everyday life. Insecurity and that uncertainty:

are born of a sense of impotence: we seem to be no longer in control, whether singly, severally or collectively – and to make things still worse we lack the tools that would allow politics to be lifted to the level where power has already settled, so enabling us to recover and repossess control over the forces shaping our shared condition.

(Bauman 2007: 26)

Bauman does not celebrate liquid modernity but regards the situation as one of interregnum. Bauman draws upon Gramsci, to explain that 'interregnum' describes a situation with the socio-political-legal order of modernity, in which the modern social order has given way to persistent and unredeemable uncertainty, but no new form of social arrangement has emerged to provide stability and markets come to underpin the constructed social order:

interregnum is a transitory state …. I intentionally selected the term interregnum to qualify our era precisely because we do not know what is at the end of the road. We know that we are on the ropes, we know what we want to get rid of, but we absolutely do not know what kind of better society we want to substitute.

(Bauman and Tablet 2017: 139)

Bauman identifies three aspects to living in the situation of interregnum. First people are troubled by their ignorance of the situation. This gives way to a feeling of impotence, people do not know what to do or how to do it. This feeling of impotence generates a feeling of inadequacy, rooted in a loss of self-confidence and the feeling of humiliation.

The stranger in solid modernity

Who is the stranger? When and how does the stranger appear? Bauman discusses the position of the stranger in solid modernity by reference to his conception of the gardening state. The solid modern state had the ambition to create a form of order that made a sharp distinction between order and chaos. Propagating preferred patterns of social life that nature was unable to provide by herself and eliminating people who did not fit the societal design. Ambivalence and strangerhood are the unwanted by-products of nation-state building. For Bauman: 'Each order has its own disorders; each model of purity has its own dirt that needs to be swept away' (Bauman 1997: 11).

In the solid modern world, the presence of the stranger brings about an unusual interruption of the routine because the stranger does not share the local assumptions and as such strangers were assumed to undermine the security upon which daily life rests. Strangers spoil the harmony, are 'out of place' and seen to be an obstacle to the purity or proper 'organisation of environment'. Strangers do not accept *our* way of life, they may question, challenge or even encourage a dismantling of the 'traditional' order and make *us* think about the way we do things around here. Strangers are often compared to vermin or bacteria and are often judged to be the carriers of disease; as such there were often calls for the stranger to be banished to protect health and maintain the preservation of social order. Anxiety is transformed into the fear of 'doing something' about the stranger, as the fear of the stranger permeates 'the totality of daily life – fills every nook and cranny of the human condition' (Bauman 1997: 11). The stranger was identified as a category of other people, who become 'dirt' and were treated as such.

Within solid modernity, nation states were said by Bauman to seek out engineering solutions to the problem of the stranger. The strangers are the wild and uncultivated elements within the population. In the same way that weeds are the waste of gardening, the uninvited guests that disrupt the garden design, ambivalence and strangerhood are waste created by the solid modern state's attempt to create order. The gardening state is about encouraging the useful plants as determined by the gardener's design and excluding weeds and other forms of waste. To support this view Bauman quotes biologist Erwin Bauer, and Bauer's colleagues at the Kaiser Wilhelm Institute for Breeding Research, Martin Stammler and Konrad Lorenz who all echoed Frederick the Great's comment:

> It annoys me to see how much trouble is taken to cultivate pine-apples, bananas and other exotic plants in this rough climate, when so little care is given to the human race. Whatever people say, a

human being is more valuable than all the pineapples in the world. He is the plant we must breed, he deserves all our trouble and care, for he is the ornament and the glory of the Fatherland.

(Bauman 1991: 27)

Bauman also cites R. W. Darre, who was to become the Nazi Minister of Agriculture:

He who leaves the plants in a garden to themselves will soon find to his surprise that the garden is overgrown by weeds and that even the basic character of the plants has changed. If therefore the garden is to remain the breeding ground for the plants, if, in other words, it is to lift itself above the harsh rule of natural forces, then the forming will of a gardener is necessary, a gardener who, by providing suitable conditions for growing, or by keeping harmful influences away, or by both together, carefully tends what needs tending, and ruthlessly eliminates the weeds which would deprive the better plants of nutrition, air, light and sun ... Thus we are facing the realization that questions of breeding are not trivial for political thought, but that they have to be at the centre of all considerations ... We must even assert that a people can only reach spiritual and moral equilibrium if a well conceived breeding plan stands at the very centre of its culture.

(cited in Bauman 1991: 27)

Under solid modernity strangers were intrinsically viewed as an anomaly to be corrected or repaired. If possible those people who did not fit the design would be assimilated. Bauman explains that: 'Chaos is the waste accumulating in the production of order' (Bauman 1991: 100). The stranger falls outside of the created order of modernity and strangerhood is the unwanted by-product of the imposition of order: 'in the same way that weeds are the products of garden designs. They have no other meaning but someone's refusal to tolerate them' (Bauman 1991: 100). In solid modernity, the state defined what the social order should look like and legislated to define divisions, classifications and boundaries into which 'the modern strangers did not fit' (Bauman 1997: 18).

Drawing on Levi-Strauss, Bauman (1997) outlines two complementary strategies that have been used by the solid modern state when dealing with the presence of strangers; first the anthropophagic approach or the strategy of *assimilation* or *conformity*. This approach involves attempting to remove what is different about the stranger and encouraging the stranger to adopt ways of thinking and acting that are like those of the locals; asking the stranger to reject their own cultural traditions, language and loyalties.

On the face of it, the liberal message of assimilation sounds like a call to end stigma, because it appears to challenge the ascriptive nature of inferiority. However, the task of 'homogenising' reinforces the position of the stranger as a defective object and reaffirms the authority of the nation state as the body responsible for fulfilling the designing/ordering/gardening ambitions of modernity. The message of assimilation demands that the state should deal with the problem of the stranger.

The second strategy Bauman identifies is described as *anthropoemic* or the strategy of exclusion – this is the imposition of prohibitions such as confining the strangers within ghettos or expelling the strangers beyond the nation state's territory. In the case of Nazi Germany when neither of the two measures was seen to be feasible or acceptable, the anthropoemic strategy became one of physically destroying the strangers.

Bauman (1991) makes a distinction between friends and enemies who are mirror reflections of each other and are brought into existence through struggle. In contrast, strangers are neither friends nor 'straightforward' enemies. The ambivalence of the stranger undermines our sense of certainty and generates doubt. As such reaction to the stranger is mainly 'negative' in Bauman's analysis. The stranger invokes a confused status, there is no rule in terms of how to behave in relation to the stranger. Friends and enemies come to learn each other's methods of classification. The stranger threatens the stable relation of opposition between friend and enemy; for Bauman, the presence of the stranger generates uncertainty and threatens even the possibility of sociation by disrupting the cognitive classificatory clarity that exists between friends and enemies. The stranger is not simply a person who has yet to learn the local ways of doing things in the way that local people do; rather the stranger is an uninvited guest, a person who is no longer 'far away', who lives in our lifeworld but remains unfamiliar:

> There is hardly an anomaly more anomalous than the stranger. He
> stands between friend and enemy, order and chaos, the inside and
> the outside. He stands for the treacherousness of friends, for the
> cunning disguise of the enemies, for fallibility of order, vulner-
> ability of the inside.
>
> *(Bauman 1991: 61)*

However, Bauman's solid modern stranger is not identical with the
Other nor the Foreigner; anybody who disrupts the social order can
become the stranger. The strangers are perceived to be ambivalent; a
condition described by Bauman as one: 'with no desirable solution,
with no foolproof choice, no unreflective knowledge of "how to go
on"' (Bauman 1991: 244–245). The strangers lack intelligibility as they
do not respond to social pressures as do the rest or act according to the
rational intelligibility of life that solid modern people take for granted.
Meursault, for example, the central character and narrator in Albert
Camus's *The Stranger* (1942) is deeply estranged. Not only is he socially
awkward, refusing to pretend to have feelings that he does not have
and refusing to conform to the customary ways of behaving on hearing
the news of the death of his mother, but he lacks any understanding of
why people find his absence of any emotional engagement odd. He is
as indifferent to his mother's death as he is indifferent to the death of
the man he murdered on the beach. The court regards the murder
simply as a pretext to convict and execute Meursault for living his life as
a stranger; for his refusal to conform. In the case of Nazi Germany, in
addition to Jews a wide range of people were identified and classified as
not fitting into the garden design, for example: gay men, promiscuous
women, prostitutes, Roma and other travellers, alcoholics, Jehovah's
Witnesses, Communists, people with a range of physical impairments
and additional learning needs.

Anyone can become cast as a stranger. The mechanisms of estrangement appear in the life of a person. The estrangement of Gregor Samsa,
the central character in Franz Kafka's novella *The Metamorphosis* is a
good example of how the process of estrangement presents itself in
individual terms: 'One morning, upon awakening from agitated
dreams, Gregor Samsa found himself, in his bed, transformed into a
monstrous vermin' (Kafka 2009/1915: 11).

Gregor wakes up to discover he has turned into a giant insect. However none of the characters in the novella seeks an explanation as to what brought about Gregor's transformation; as such the transformation appears to be without cause or reason. Moreover, Gregor himself never attempts to find out how or why he was transformed. Kafka presents Gregor as the victim of an evidently purposeless and random metamorphosis, which is the product of context in which irrational and chaotic things happen without our full understanding.

As we saw with Simmel's and Derrida's reading of *The Metamorphosis*, the metaphor of the door is central to Kafka's unfolding narrative. In the first part of the story when Gregor is still attempting to turn over and open the door, the transformation totally changes his appearance, and although Gregor is unable to communicate his thoughts and feelings to his family, his sense of who he is remains unchanged. Once the door is opened his family develops a psychological distance towards him and even his sister's initial feelings of sympathy turn to revulsion towards him. Gregor becomes excluded and eventually accepts his separation from humanity.

What can be taken from this reading of Gregor's transformation is the assumption that strangeness and the precarity is experienced personally, the mechanisms that bring the situation about are often not identified, not questioned but exclude individuals to the degree that even family members may not regard the stranger as fully human.

Stigma is used as a weapon against the unwelcome ambiguity of the stranger. If we were to come across the stranger, this encounter will often in Martin Buber's terms take the form of vergegnung rather than begegnung. Vergegnung is described by Buber (1970/1923) as a 'mismeeting', a form of encountering with the Other in which there is no trust or real interactive mutuality between the persons. An encounter in which our perception of the Other is rooted in stereotypes, misrepresentation and misunderstanding rather than based upon a coming together that is both personal and reciprocal.

The stranger in postmodernity

Postmodernity for Bauman (1991) means first and foremost a recognition and appreciation of the enduring plurality of the social world. In postmodern times men and women live continuously with what

Bauman calls the 'identity problem'. By this Bauman means that people do not want an 'identity for life' and reject sameness, but they are concerned that they may lack the resources to build and maintain a flexible identity that allows them to engage with their chosen life pursuits and be able to resist or navigate the external forces of the market place. In the postmodern condition, the problem of identity is one of avoiding a fixed identity, avoiding long-term commitments, consistency and devotion. In place of a life project established as early as possible, that we loyally keep to, postmodern people who want to keep their options open choose to have a series of short projects that are not fixed. The nature of postmodernity is described by Bauman as the 'postmodern habitat'; an unpredictable 'complex system' generated by human agents from their own random movements, a form of *sociality* rather than *society* that is both undetermined and determining and contains no notion of progress in the modern sense of the word. There are no goal-setting, managing or coordinating institutions within the complex system; this makes constraint fall to an absolute minimum. Therefore, the human agent or any other element cannot be discussed by reference to its functionality or dysfunctionality; and no one agency can determine the activity of any other agent. The postmodern world has the feel of being in a continuous present. Postmodern fear is the fear 'that freedom is under threat and may be lost' (Bauman 1997: 27). In the postmodern condition, in a world made up of shopping malls, Disneylands, individual enjoyment and consumer choice, there is, argues Bauman, an 'acceptance of irredeemable plurality of the world' and a 'widespread aversion to grand social designs' and 'Strangerhood has become universal. Or, rather, it has been dissolved; which, after all, amounts to the same. If everyone is a stranger, no one is' (Bauman 1991: 97).

Bauman continues: 'This is now a late-modern, or postmodern, world of universal particularity; a world integrated through its diversity, little worried by difference and resigned to ambiguity' (Bauman 1991: 161).

In the postmodern world, it is not necessarily that case that strangers were intrinsically viewed as an anomaly to be corrected or repaired (Bauman 1997: 19). Bauman explains that 'the postmodern eye (that is, the modern eye liberated from modern fears and inhibitions) views difference with zest and glee: difference is beautiful and no less good for that' (Bauman 1991: 255). This situation has come about within the postmodern condition, argues Bauman, because there has been a:

> blurring and the watering down of the difference between the normal and the abnormal, the expectable and the unexpected, the ordinary and the bizarre, domesticated and wild – the familiar and the strange, 'us' and the strangers. The strangers are no longer authoritatively preselected, defined and set apart, as they used to be in times of the state-managed, consistent and durable programmes of order-building.
>
> *(Bauman 1997: 25)*

However, Bauman does argue that postmodernity is generally weak on exclusion. Postmodern men and women fear that they may lose the ability or the resources to build an identity around the pleasurable, sensory experience and chosen life pursuits, which generates a fear of becoming 'slimy'. Taking his starting point from Mary Douglas's conception of clean or dirty and her sociological reading of Jean-Paul Sartre's analysis of *le visqueux*, Bauman explores what it means to be slimy:

> Only at the very moment when I believe that I possess it, behold by a curious reversal, it possesses me … If an object which I hold in my hands is solid, I can let go when I please; its inertia symbolizes for me my total power … Yet here is the slimy reversing the terms; [my self] is suddenly compromised, I open my hands, I want to let go of the slimy and it sticks to me, it draws me, it sucks at me … I am no longer the master … The slime is like a liquid seen in a nightmare, where all its properties are animated by a sort of life and turn back against me … If I dive into the water, if I plunge into it, if I let myself sink in it, I experience no discomfort, for I do not have any fear whatsoever that I may dissolve in it; I remain a solid in its liquidity. If I sink in the slimy, I feel that I am going to be lost in it … To touch the slimy is to risk being dissolved in sliminess.
>
> *(Sartre 1969: 608–610 cited in Bauman 1997: 26–27)*

Drawing upon a liquid metaphor, Bauman suggests that postmodern women and men, as pleasure-seeking consumers, enjoy the feeling of alterity when they their draw upon their skills and resources and engage in swimming in the exhilarating sea-water of the life world. However, if the substance that they find themselves in has more in common with resin, tar, honey or treacle, the substance will stick to the skin, and what follows is sliminess, loss of mastery and dependency. The less that people can control their lives the more they come to be resented both by themselves and others. The more a person is perceived to be slimy the more that form of alterity will be something to be disentangled from and the more frantically will be the attempt by postmodern women and men to exclude the slimy. Unlike other forms of difference, powerlessness, the inability to exercise choice, is seen as a trap and not as an 'adventure park'. The polarisation within the postmodern world is a product of the process of individualisation and the inability to engage with, for with the seductive powers of the consumer market: 'The sliminess of strangers, let us repeat, is the reflection of their own powerlessness' (Bauman 1997: 29).

Powerlessness is seen by the postmoderns as a personal failing that leads to privation and sliminess and although difference remains something to be celebrated, postmoderns want to detach themselves from the contaminating sliminess of strangers: 'the preferable mode of living with strangers is to keep apart' (Bauman 1997: 31) by erecting mini-Berlin Walls; protective walls of playful unconcern

> to maintain distance and to separate ... At one pole, strangehood (and difference in general) will go on being constructed as the source of pleasurable experience and aesthetic satisfaction; at the other, as the terrifying incarnation of the unstoppably rising sliminess of the human condition – as the effigy for all future ritual burning of its horrors.
>
> *(Bauman 1997: 33–34)*

For Bauman, the postmodern condition has divided society into the happy seduced and the unhappy oppressed. Bauman (1998) explores more fully the ideas of the slimy postmodern stranger as a flawed consumer. The postmodern condition is a form of social formation ruled by the aesthetic of consumption, and contains a form of market-promoted tolerance in which the condition of 'being poor' no longer means 'being unemployed', but being a flawed consumer, a person who is redundant – not wanted because of their own personal and individual misfortune rooted in the lack of the skills, abilities and resources to enjoy the consumer market place. The redundant flawed consumers are seen to be without a useful social function or chance of improvement:

> Each flawed consumer licks his or her wounds in solitude, at best in the company of their as yet unbroken family and mostly similarly resourceless friends. Flawed consumers are lonely and feel abandoned, and when they are left lonely for a long time they tend to become loners; they do not see how society can help, they do not hope to be helped, they do not believe that their lot can be changed by anything but football pools or a lottery win.
>
> *(Bauman 1998: 115)*

The stranger in liquid modernity

In Bauman's analysis of the postmodern stranger he moves away from the conceptual understanding of the stranger as a newcomer, a member of a minority facing the majority. The presence of the stranger reminds the locals of the constructed nature of the culture. The Us and Them schema is no longer useful in the postmodern condition. People who choose to cross borders could be pilgrims, tourists or vagabonds (Bauman 1993) but movement across a border did not in itself define a person as a stranger. The problem of postmodern strangerhood was subsumed within issues related to the complexity of identity, consumption, taste, style and life politics. From Bauman's sociology of postmodernity to his liquid turn writings there is a qualitative shift in his understanding of the nature and content of strangerhood. Like postmodernity, liquid modernity is characterised by a rampant individualisation in which people are viewed as responsible for the actions that they take in response to global forces that present themselves. This generates a new form of precarity. In postmodernity, we are all strangers to some degree some of the time and strangerhood was to be admired, even celebrated. The successful inhabitants or the denizens of the liquid modernity world are the people described by Simmel (1950/

1908) as the urban strollers, or later by Baudelaire and Foucault as the *flaneurs*. Such people became 'the central symbolic figure of the modern city' (Bauman 1996: 26), the metropolitan who gazes at the surface meaning of things in the cosmopolitan urban environment and has no real concern for the deeper meaning underneath the surface of anything. As in the postmodern world, so in the liquid modern world, the shopping mall is the place where we are most likely to see the flaneurs. In contrast, in liquid modernity strangers are foreigners and strangerhood is above all linked to refugee or illegal migrant status; such people are intruders rather than guests and their company is not wanted. If possible, their entry will be refused and if they manage to gain entry it is against our will and their presence will not be celebrated.

Cities have become the dumping grounds in which the problems generated by globalisation, including people who are displaced, are placed by global conflict. Bauman (2010) identifies three distinct patterns of migration over the course of modernity. The first phase is rooted in a 'gardening posture' in which Europeans moved into what were considered to be 'empty lands' to secure economic advantages. The native populations were driven from their lands. The second phase of migration is what Bauman refers to as the 'Empire Strikes Back': as colonialism becomes dismantled many colonial residents follow their former colonial leaders back to Europe again to secure economic advantage for themselves and their families.

The current phase of migration has its roots in a 'globalization-induced logic of planetary redistribution of life resources' (Bauman 2010: 150). There is no connection between the migrants' territorially determined identity, citizenship and place. The newly arrived migrants often require the skills to be able to participate in our art of living. In liquid modernity, the processes of globalisation have brought about a breakdown in the global division between 'centre' and 'periphery' – between 'developed' and 'underdeveloped' parts of the world. Consequently, people are on the move and refugees are defined as human waste. The refugees are: 'the outsiders incarnate' (Bauman 2004: 80). The refugees are identified as people: 'with no useful function to play in the land of their arrival and temporary stay and no intention or prospect of being assimilated and incorporated into the new social body' (Bauman 2004: 77). Refugees are classed as 'being under protection' but this does not mean 'being wanted': 'and everything needed, and much more, is being done to prevent the refugees from confusing the two conditions' (Bauman 2004: 79). Refugees are classed as 'being under protection' until: 'the powers-that-be decide that the exiles are no longer refugees since "it is safe to return" to homeland that has long ceased to be their homeland' (Bauman 2004: 79).

When the redundant humans are already 'inside' they are pushed into urban ghettoes or 'hyperghettoes' – dumping grounds for those for whom the surrounding society has no economic or political use (Bauman 2004: 81). The hyperghetto is seen as a:

> single-purpose, waste disposal tip …. A one-dimensional machinery for naked relegation, a human warehouse, wherein are discarded those segments of urban society deemed disreputable, derelict, and dangerous … prisonlike Goffmanesque 'total institutions': a 'prisonization' of public housing ever more reminiscent of houses of detention.
>
> *(Bauman 2004: 82)*

The social state is gradually but relentlessly and consistently turned into a 'garrison state' and: 'Social problems are increasingly criminalised' in which 'Repression increases and replaces compassion' (Bauman 2004: 85).

Bauman's conception of the stranger in liquid modernity, unlike in solid modernity and postmodernity, is focused on geographical territory and a sense of physical location; what he calls 'corridors of exile' such as refugee camps, encampments of the homeless and urban ghettos: 'Legal or illegal residents of all these places share one decisive trait: they are all redundant. Rejects or the refuse of society. In a nutshell, waste' (Bauman 2012: 159).

Bauman (2002) argues that throughout modern history, nation states accepted migrants fleeing from other sovereign powers. Today such migrants are viewed as nomads, but not by choice, they move because of fate and are seen by Bauman as the 'collateral victims' of global forces. These nomads continue to be viewed as strangers and their presence at our door is a 'cause of anxiety precisely because of being strange'. 'Stateless persons' are a product of modern state sovereignty and the management of tightly controlled borders and the prevention of uncontrolled human movements: 'Passports, entry and exit visas, and customs and immigration controls were prime inventions of the art of modern government' (Bauman 2003: 125). Human rights are institutionally rooted within the concept of 'place' and as such the state boundary classifies people as either citizens or foreigners. If a foreigner has no legitimate reason to cross the border, if they lack passports, entry or exit visas, the boundary between citizens and foreigners becomes a boundary between the human with rights and the inhuman without: 'The ultimate sanction of the modern sovereign power turned out to be the right of exemption from humanity' (Bauman 2003: 126). Intolerance towards the stranger becomes more nationalist in orientation as national boundaries are perceived as being transgressed and can become especially ugly when local differences are seen to be under threat:

> Sharing a table with 'strangers', frequenting places known as the abode and domain of outsiders, to say nothing of romances and marriages with partners from beyond the boundaries of the community, become marks of betrayal and a justification for ostracism and exile.
>
> *(Bauman 2011: 68)*

Liquid moderns seek active avoidance of contact with the stranger because of the fear of contamination from those who are not like 'us' but who are at *our* door. Hostility is directed towards everything associated with the stranger's way of life:

> their ways of talking, their ways of dressing, their rituals, the way they organize their family life and even the smell of the food they like to cook. Layered upon this is their apparent refusal to engage in the natural order of social relations and so they do not accept responsibility, as 'we' have to do, for their actions.
>
> *(Bauman and May 2001: 38)*

Taking his starting point from an observation that Kant made in 1784, Bauman (2003) notes that because the Earth is a sphere, wherever the unwanted migrants go will become frontier land and this will become the place where the barrier will be constructed between the locals and the strangers. When all places are occupied without hospitality the migrants are forced to move from one unwelcoming place to another. Everywhere the migrants go becomes frontier land. Being human does not in itself provide a person with rights; stateless people cannot claim to be equal before the law simply because are not covered by the law. The migrant becomes suspended in the spatial void of the refugee camp, a form of 'frozen transience' or a 'lasting state of temporariness' in which they are neither motionless nor wanderers:

> The sole meaning of being an insider of a refugee camp is to be an outsider, a stranger, an alien body, an intruder in the rest of the world; in short, evicted from the world shared by the rest of humanity.
>
> *(Bauman 2012: 158–159)*

Socially the migrant becomes like a 'zombie' with their old identity surviving only as does a ghost. They share the fate described by Jacques Derrida as 'undecidables'; unthinkables, unimaginables, untouchables. This is an important point for Bauman, which he has emphasised on several occasions:

> In the habitual terms in which human identities are narrated, they are ineffable. They are Jacques Derrida's 'undecidables' made flesh. Among people like us, praised by others and priding ourselves for the arts of reflection and self-reflection, they are not only untouchables, but unthinkables. In a world filled to the brim with imagined communities, they are the unimaginables. And it is by refusing them the right to be imagined that the others, assembled in genuine or hoping-to-become-genuine communities, seek credibility for their own labours of the imagination.
>
> *(Bauman 2003: 141; Bauman 2007: 45–46)*

They are Jacques Derrida's 'undecidables' made flesh. Among people like us, praised by others and priding ourselves on arts of reflection and selfreflection, they are not only untouchables, but unthinkables. In our world of imagined communities, they are the

unimaginables. And it is by refusing them the right to be imagined
that the other – genuine or hoping-to-become-genuine communities, seek credibility for their own labours of the imagination.

(Bauman 2002: 108)

Moreover, there is a significant difference between the experience
of being a stranger in a stable and established world, and the
experience of strangerhood in an unstable world. The condition of
being a stranger is no longer a temporary condition; rootlessness for
many has become a universal condition. Strangers are not like us
and not like the people we interact with, cohabit with, our neighbours. The sudden appearance of strangers whom we did not invite
and were not consulted about: 'is a major cause of anxiety and fear'
(Bauman 2016: 8–9). Strangers are: '"harbingers of bad news". They
are embodiments of the collapse of order' (Bauman 2016: 15):

In addition to representing the 'great unknown' all strangers
embody, the refugees bring home distant noises of war and the
stench of gutted homes and scorched towns that cannot but
remind the established how easily the cocoon of safe and familiar
(safe because familiar) routine may be pierced or crushed.

(Bauman 2002: 115)

Strangers are nomads whose movement is brought about by: 'global,
distant, occasionally heard about but mostly unseen, intangible,
obscure, mysterious and not easy to imagine forces, powerful
enough to interfere also with our lives while neglecting and ignor-
ing our own preferences' (Bauman 2016: 16), as liquid moderns
continue to define themselves within a geographical location and as
having the 'rights of belonging' that are denied to the stranger.
Liquid moderns object to the uninvited and obtrusive proximity of
strangers, bringing about a drive to protect the homogeneous, territorially isolated environment:

Strangers tend to appear ever more frightening as they become
increasingly 'strange' – alien, unfamiliar and incomprehensible – and
as the mutual communication which could eventually assimilate their

'otherness' to one's own lifeworld loses substance and fades, or never takes off in the first place.

(Bauman 2011: 64)

To be seen to respond to such global forces, governments subject the nomadic strangers to forms of 'securitization'. Echoing his earlier argument, Bauman suggests that once inside the host country the migrants were subjected to one of two approaches to minimise their strangeness; either the anthropohagic solution, which involved subjecting the stranger to a form of power-assisted assimilation, or alternatively the anthropoemic solution, rounding up the strangers and expelling them. However, for Bauman in the liquid modern world, neither of these approaches: 'commands much credibility today ... and so the chances of deploying either of the two orthodox strategies are, to say the least, slim' (Bauman 2002: 111). Instead, governments attempt to close the doors, restricting the right to asylum and refusing entry to refugees and 'economic migrants'. Post 9/11 migrants are often viewed as potentially a terrorist threat; people who are both risky and more likely to be at risk.

Bauman explains that one of the most disturbing effects of globalisation is the deregulation of wars. A condition that has increased significantly the number of people who find themselves in war zones and victims between warring factions. Such people must move away from places that they had previously called home. Migrants have become the precarite, people whose fears and anxieties come from been caught in a double bind, caught in the cross-fire, non-combatants in somebody else's conflict, in a psychological impasse caused by having lost their place in the world after fleeing one place but denied entry to any other: 'Refugees are the very embodiment of "human waste"' (Bauman 2007: 41). Wherever they go they are made to feel unwanted. In liquid modernity refugees are stripped of every part of their identities except their status as a refugee; subjected to bio-segregation, stateless and outside of the law, refugees often find themselves in a situation of 'liminal drift' with no authority to which their statehood could point to. The refugee no longer has access to the resources to build an identity, and finds their identity defined and constructed around images of barbed wire, security guards and camps: '"asylum seekers" have now replaced the evil-eyed witches and other unrepentant evildoers, the malignant spooks and hobgoblins of former urban legends' (Bauman 2007: 43). Having lost any legitimate right to a 'place', the refugees find themselves inhabiting what Marc Augé describes as a non-place, Joel Garreau's nowherevilles and Michel Foucault's Narrenschiff.

Marc Augé on the non-place

The starting point for Marc Augé's analysis of the non-place is a distinction that Merleau-Ponty (1965/1945) makes in *Phenomenologie de la perception* between 'geometric' space (how we see things in the world with perception coming from the phenomenal field rather than from the categories of the mind) and 'anthropological space' (a space that incorporates all human activity and is not reduced to a physical location alone). For Augé, our experience of society is in time and space, but it is also the experience of belonging to that society or not. Culture and individuality are identified as reciprocal expressions of one another. An individual is not just anybody; the individual is identified with the society of which she or he is an expression. A person's individuality for Augé is a synthesis, and an expression of a culture. Symbolic universes constitute a means of recognition by collections of codes that the indigenous people who share the culture accept. Individuals and groups inside the culture define themselves in terms of the same criteria. As such other cultures seem very different when they are read through: 'the ethnocentric grille of their own customary behaviour' (Augé 1995: 35). 'Anthropological place' is formed by individual identities, through complicities of language, local references, the unformulated rules of living know-how; non-place creates the shared identity of passengers, customers or Sunday drives' (Augé 1995: 100).

Anthropological place is a location in which there is a social demarcation of the soil and the historical by 'collectivities' of people who recognise themselves as:

> indigenous inhabitants who live in it, cultivate it, defend it, mark its strong points and keep its frontiers under surveillance, but who also detect in it the traces of chthonian or celestial powers, ancestors or spirits which populate and animate its private geography.
>
> *(Augé 1995: 42)*

Within the anthropological place the indigenous inhabitants draw a clear frontier: 'between the zone of relative identity (recognised identity and established relations) and the external world, a world of absolute foreignness' (Augé 1995: 50). Within this place the indigenous inhabitants need to:

> symbolize the components of shared identity (shared by the whole of a group), particular identity (of a given group or individual in relation to others) and singular identity (what makes the individual or group of individuals different from any other).
>
> *(Augé 1995: 51)*

To have a sense of 'anthropological place' is to feel assigned to residence; something that provides a meaning and intelligibility for the people who live within the space. The material and visible frontier is then a constituent of individual identity.

However, within supermodernity culture has experienced a process of de-localisation:

> never before have individual histories been so explicitly affected by collective history, but never before, either, have the reference points for collective identification been so unstable. The individual production of meaning is thus more necessary than ever
>
> *(Augé 1995: 37)*

> If a place can be defined as relational, historical and concerned with identity, then a space which cannot be defined as relational, or historical, or concerned with identity will be a non-place. The hypothesis advanced here is that supermodernity produces non-places, meaning spaces which are not themselves anthropological places.
>
> *(Augé 1995: 77–78)*

The non-place is a space of contemporary consumption; hotel chains, leisure parks, large retail outlets, and above all the traveller's space such as the airport departure lounge is the epitome of the non-place. Non-places are spaces in which neither identity nor relations make any sense. A person who enters the non-place becomes no more than what she or he does or experiences such as the role of commuter or customer. For many people who feel that they their life is rigidly governed, the comparative lack of restriction in the non-place can be experienced as a form of liberation: 'the passive joys of identity-loss'. However, entry into the non-place is a contractual one. You need a ticket, passport, visa or proof of purchase to enter and leave the non-place and as such there is no individualisation (and as such no right to anonymity) without identity checks:

> The passenger through non-places retrieves his identity only at Customs, at the tollbooth, at the check-out counter. Meanwhile, he obeys the same code as others, receives the same messages, responds to the same entreaties. The space of non-place creates neither singular identity nor-relations; only solitude and similitude.
>
> *(Augé 1995: 103)*

Non-places deal only with individuals as customers, passengers, users, listeners; identified by name, occupation, place of birth and address only on entering or leaving the space. 'A paradox of non-place: a for-eigner lost in a country he does not know (a "passing stranger") can feel at home there only in the anonymity of motorways, service stations, big stores or hotel chains' (Augé 1995: 106).

In the supermodernity, non-places interconnect and fit together in such a way that people are always but never really at home and what were once believed to be frontier zones no longer provide a vision of completely unknown or unfamiliar spaces. 'Elsewhere' is no longer recognised or understood as a singular and distinct (exotic) object: 'The non-place is the opposite of utopia: it exists, and it does not contain any organic society' (Augé 1995: 111–112). Non-place is a space without the 'gravitational pull of place and tradition'. Entering non-places is what Augé describes as an experience: 'without real historical pre-cedent – of solitary individuality combined with non-human mediation (all it takes is a notice or a screen) between the individual and the public authority' (Augé 1995: 117–118).

Joel Garreau (1991) describes 'edge cities' as 'nowherevilles'; a parti-cular form of non-place that has little if any connection with the physical location in which it has developed. Such non-places are characterised by contemporary mirrored-glass offices, accompanied by well-appointed gardens, shopping malls that contain shops that are found in other malls globally, a night-time economy including chain restaurants that are also found in malls globally, cinema chains showing films with a global appeal, near to airports and with extensive parking. They are places of white-collar work, retail and recreation. Refugee camps have much in common with the non-places or 'nowherevilles' that dominate the urban environment in that they are characterised by extra territoriality, not truly belonging of the place that they physically occupy.

Narrenschiff

Foucault (1965) describes how in the middle ages an uneasiness emerged in relation to the position of mad people within the commu-nity; the mad became increasingly viewed as dangerous figures who were a threat to the community. Narrenschiff refers to a medieval process of expelling mad people from the community by placing them on ships and launching them into the Rhine and Flemish canals. Nar-renschiff is central to the argument developed by Michel Foucault (1965) in *Madness and Civilization*. Placing mad people onto ships and launching them not only excluded the mad but placed them in a lim-inal position; drifting into a liminal space. Modern asylum seekers can be viewed as a contemporary version of the Narrenschiffen, often por-trayed as a danger or threat that must be denied entry, expelled or detained. Although no longer placed onto 'ships of fools', refugees find themselves forced into what Michel Agier (2002) terms a state of 'frozen transience', in other words in refugee camps that are in a long-term state of continuing temporariness.

The liquid modern stranger, Bauman argues, is in a state of perma-nent liminality. The liminal experience (van Gennep 1960/1908; Turner 1967, 1969) is characterised or associated with transgression; the conventions that were once regarded as fixed and secure become weak and vulnerable. On a wider societal level, liminality emerges during a period of interregnum; historical phases of social and cultural transition when the stability and repetitive aspects of social relations are broken but are yet to be replaced.

The 'migrant problem' has come to be viewed not as an ethical issue but as a problem of national and personal security. Securitization reduces the opportunities for face to face encounters between migrants and the population on the other side of the door. Securitization not only stigmatises the migrant; securitization reinforces the view that the stranger is potentially dangerous, as such, the stranger is subjected to forms of dehumanisation that invite us to place the migrant outside of our moral responsibility. The suffering of the migrant is not on our conscience because for Bauman securitization leads to adiaphorisation: 'the exemption of certain categories of other humans from the realm of moral obligation' (Bauman 2016: 83).

In *This Is Not A Diary*, Bauman (2012) takes his starting point from Norbert Elias's (2008) argument in *Established versus Outsiders*; the strangers are people that resist assimilation and classification:

> The 'established': people settled in an area of the city who suddenly see a growing number of unfamiliar faces on the street, of people strangely dressed, behaving peculiarly, talking incomprehensibly – in short, of 'outsiders' who 'do not belong here'. The 'outsiders': strangers – neither friends nor enemies, and so unpredictable, arousing anxiety and fear.
>
> *(Bauman 2012: 25)*

The 'established' do not know how to decode the conduct and intentions of the stranger and as such the 'established' come to feel lost and ignorant in terms of how to stave off possible danger. Consequently, the 'established' are inclined to engage in: 'Blaming the immigrants' – the strangers, the newcomers, and particularly the newcomers among the strangers – for all aspects of social malaise (and first of all for the nauseating, disempowering feeling of Unsicherheit, incertezza, précarité, insecurity)' (Bauman 2012: 28).

The stranger is viewed as ambivalent or even slimy within liquid modernity and not the object of our responsibility; liquid moderns do not recognise the stranger as having any quality or characteristic of a friend. Bauman's underpinning assumption is that that moral value of a human being is grounded in motivations that are natural to all human beings; as such Bauman advocates that people should respond to the stranger by drawing upon Levinas's response to the Other; however, in liquid modernity the stranger is de-faced and deprived of the protection that moral proximity offers: 'Deprived of ethically significant "face" by the fact of being classified as a security threat and thereby evicted from the universe of moral obligations .... Once stripped of 'face', the weakness of the Other invites violence naturally and effortlessly' (Bauman 2011: 59).

Although Bauman has made it clear that he would like to see a world characterised by 'integration without separation' (Bauman 2017: 161) and shares Pope Francis' hope for a cosmopolitically integrated humanity, he is pessimistic that the common TINA (there is no alternative) mentality can be overcome, as liquid modern people have an: 'Impulse of rejection' (Bauman 2017: 81). The mechanism of association separates us from them, 'the people unlike us' are still in place and 'them' are still 'off limits to integration' and still 'barred from crossing over' (Bauman 2017: 156).

However, there is no one event or date that Bauman identifies as the symbolic moment when the transition from solid to liquid modernity took place. Academics have focused on discussing the mechanisms that bring about the transition from solid to liquid modernity within Bauman's work but have largely ignored the meaning and content of what his comprehension of 'modernity' is within solid and liquid modernity. Although Bauman sidesteps the chore of defining 'modernity' and instead provides lists of possible characteristics, it is important to keep in mind that the word 'modernity' is not used by Bauman descriptively as an alternative to the word 'contemporary'. The retention of the concept of 'modernity' implies that 'solid' modernity and 'liquid' modernity share something in common for Bauman. Solid modernity is described as 'order-obsessed', a 'society of all-embracing, compulsory and enforced homogeneity' (Bauman 2000: 25). Maintaining order is a central role of the state in both solid and liquid modernity; excluding everything the state considers ambiguous, frightening and undesirable is a focus that remains central to the solid and liquid modern state.

Outside of vague references to global forces and the impact of the 'the new world disorder', Bauman focuses on 'who' is strange, but not necessarily how 'strangeness' occurs within liquid modernity. In an interview with Brad Evans, Bauman repeats his argument that refugees are often presented as a danger to the 'established native populations' rather than as a vulnerable part of humanity: 'By stopping them on the other side of our properly fortified borders, it is implied that we'll manage to stop those global forces that brought them to our doors.' The refugee symbolises the liquidity of fear in the contemporary world: 'Right now, at least, that liquidity creates a sort of affinity between the strangers at our doors and the mysterious, seemingly omnipotent global forces that pushed them there' (Evans and Bauman 2016)

References to 'stranger at our door', brought to our door by vague global forces and 'the new world disorder' in Bauman's conception of liquid modernity perpetuate the notion that in order to study the stranger we need to study individuals who are outsiders, or at least clearly marked off from mainstream society because they are foreign not different. The transition from the postmodern to the liquid modern stranger in Bauman's work signals his underpinning but unstated view that contemporary society is going back to modernity. A key characteristic of modernity for Bauman in both its solid and liquid forms remains social exclusion when the urge to convert is prevented. Modernity within both its solid and liquid forms contains a centralised state that is responsible for the protection of a national border from foreigners. Unlike within Bauman's sociology of postmodernity, protection from the foreigner in both solid and liquid modernity is considered a key aspect of the protection of the totality.

For Bauman, both the processes of inclusion and the processes of exclusion are central to the maintenance of any social formation. In liquid modernity, human groups continue, as they have always done, to define themselves by the exclusion of some categories of person. Liquid moderns are willing to act on their impulse of rejection (Bauman 2017: 81).

Drawing upon Putnam (2000), Bauman explains that social capital is a universal building block of social organisation. Social capital underpins the strength and resilience of our social ties and our ability to have confidence in people. Taking his starting point from Putnam (2000), Bauman differentiates between two ways of employing social capital, which he terms 'bridging' and 'bonding'. Bridging describes the attempt to achieve social advancement, and lack of bridging is an aspect of social degradation. Bonding describes the employment of social capital to bond groups and establish oneself within a group by limiting outsiders' access to the group, and excluding strangers. Social capital is for Bauman a resource that locals draw upon to both include and exclude the stranger. As Bauman explains, social capital is: 'just as crucial for throwing the gates open as it is for digging moats … it is used for both goals' (Bauman and Obirek 2015: 26). In addition, argues Bauman, all social groups: 'derive their capacity of survival from a dialectic of integration and separation … inclusion and exclusion … neither of the two processes can be entirely eliminated' (26–27). Inclusion and exclusion are, then, what Bauman and Obirek describe as two sides of the same coin: 'they cannot get by without each other'; underpinning inclusion is the 'urge to convert' the Other, whilst exclusion is the urge to leave out, reject or ignore (27).

In an interview with Thomas Leoncini (Bauman and Leoncini 2018a), Bauman was asked about his experience of bullying. Reflecting on his experiences at school, Bauman said that the Jewish boys in the school he attended were subjected to bullying. He explained that even as a child he understood that bullying was a form of exclusion. Bauman's non-Jewish classmates made it clear: 'You are not like us, you do not belong, you have no right to join our games, we won't play with you; if you insist on sharing in our life, don't be puzzled by all that beating, kicking, offending, degrading, and debasing' (Bauman and Leoncini 2018: 39). Much later he came to the conclusion that his exclusion, and that of the other Jewish boys, was a central element in the construction of the bullies' self-identification.

Conclusion

In Bauman's analysis, the word stranger is used across his conceptions of solid, post and liquid modernity. However, the meaning and content of what it means to be strange, together with Bauman's understanding of the mechanisms that bring strangerhood into existence differ considerably and are often contradictory. In solid modernity, the stranger is any individual who does not conform to the state's plan for the modern society. In this conception of the stranger any person who is seen to contradict the state's understanding of how to lead a life runs the risk of having strangerhood imposed upon them. Any person at any time can become a stranger if the state deems them to be strange. In contest, in postmodernity the ability of the state to impose order on the way people choose to lead their lives is significantly diminished. In postmodernity difference is celebrated and as such we are all strangers, and when we all are strangers none of us are strangers. The postmodern fear is that we may lack the skills and resources to participate fully in the consumer market place; we may be seen as people with bad taste rooted in personal failure and incompetence as a consumer. Such flawed consumers can be stigmatised as slimy; a form of strangerhood that is both contaminated and contaminating. Finally, in liquid modernity Bauman makes a distinction between the Other as the excluded flawed consumer who can potentially become *homo sacer*, a person who is poor, slimy and already judged as leading a life not worth living. Alternatively, there are Foreigners who are strangers; outsiders, migrants, refugees and asylum seekers. Unlike previous interpretations of the stranger, Bauman's (2016) liquid modern stranger is a racial category, a person from far away who is an uninvited guest and whose presence is neither wanted nor desired.

In Bauman's analysis of the postmodern stranger he moves away from the conceptual understanding of the stranger as a newcomer, a member of a minority facing the majority. The presence of the stranger reminds the locals of the constructed nature of the culture; but movement across a border does not in itself define a person as a stranger. The problem of postmodern strangerhood was subsumed within issues related to the complexity of identity, consumption, taste, style and life politics. For Bauman, the stranger in liquid modernity is a migrant, a person who is not 'like us' and threatening. The liquid modern stranger is a newcomer who cannot be assimilated and remains marginal. Like Simmel's stranger, Bauman's conception of the liquid modern stranger is focused on movement across geographical territory and soil; the conception is rooted in a sense of physical location. Bauman's conception of the stranger in liquid modernity is essentially focused on spatial movement, and forms of spatial foreignness. The liquid modern stranger becomes part of a nameless, impersonal mass. The strangeness of strangers is ambivalent, discomforting and frightening. The conditions for the emergence of the stranger are rooted in impersonal global forces and dispossession. Liquid modern strangerhood is a product of structural inequalities; a product of a general shift in how society deals with the presence of migrants. The liquid modern stranger is a menacing new-comer who cannot be a member of the community; a person who unlike the locals is not bound to the soil. Unlike his conception of postmodern strangerhood that incorporated a rich variety of forms of social, sexual and cultural behavioural performances that are associated with Otherness, Bauman's liquid modern stranger is socially organised, defined and externalised as a foreigner. The discussion of the stranger in liquid modernity in Bauman's work raises the question of the transition from post to liquid modernity and why postmodernity no longer pro-vides an adequate foundation for explaining the nature of con-temporary strangerhood. Outside of vague references to global forces, Bauman focuses on 'who' is strange, but not necessarily how 'strange-ness' occurs within liquid modernity. The discussion of the stranger in liquid modernity in Bauman's work raises the question of the transition from post to liquid modernity and why postmodernity no longer pro-vides an adequate foundation for explaining the nature of con-temporary strangerhood. Why does not 'like us' become defined in relation to geographical territory and soil within liquid modernity in terms of defining strangeness when territory and soil is irrelevant in postmodernity?

References

Agier, M. (2002) Between war and city: Towards an urban anthropology of refugee camps, *Ethnography*, 3(3), 361–366.

Augé, M. (1995) *Non-places: Introduction to an anthropology of supermodernity*, trans. J. Howe. London: Verso.

Bauman, Z. (1991) *Modernity and ambivalence*. Oxford: Blackwell.

Bauman, Z. (1993) *Postmodern ethics*. Oxford: Blackwell.

Bauman, Z. (1996) *Alone again: Ethics after certainty*. London: Demos.

Bauman, Z. (1997) *Postmodernity and its discontents*. Cambridge: Polity.

Bauman, Z. (1998) *Work, consumerism and the new poor*. Maidenhead: Open University Press.

Bauman, Z. (2000) *Liquid modernity*. Cambridge: Polity.

Bauman, Z. (2002) *Society under siege*. Cambridge: Polity.

Bauman, Z. (2003) *Liquid love: On the frailty of human bonds*. Cambridge: Polity.

The camps and the stranger 105

Bauman, Z. (2004) *Wasted lives: Modernity and its outcasts*. Cambridge: Polity.

Bauman, Z. (2007) *Liquid times: Living in an age of uncertainty*. Cambridge: Polity.

Bauman, Z. (2010) *44 Letters from the liquid modern world*. Cambridge: Polity.

Bauman, Z. (2011) *Collateral damage*. Cambridge: Polity.

Bauman, Z. (2012) *This is not a diary*. Cambridge: Polity.

Bauman, Z. (2016) *Strangers at our door*. Cambridge: Polity.

Bauman, Z. (2017) *Retrotopia*. Cambridge: Polity.

Bauman, Z. and Leoncini, T. (2018) *Born liquid: Transformations in the third millennium*. Cambridge: Polity.

Bauman, Z. and Leoncini, T. (2018a) 'Evil has been trivialized': A final conversation with Zygmunt Bauman https://www.nybooks.com/daily/2018/12/06/evil-has-been-trivialized-a-final-conversation-with-zymunt-bauman/

Bauman, Z. and May, T. (2001) *Thinking sociologically*. Oxford: Blackwell.

Bauman, Z. and Obirek, S. (2015) *Of God and man*. Cambridge: Polity.

Bauman, Z. and Tablet, S. (2017) Interview with Zygmunt Bauman: From the modern project to the liquid world. *Theory, Culture & Society*, 34(7/8), 131–146.

Buber, M. (1970/1923) *I and thou*. New York: Charles Scribner's Sons.

Elias, N. (2008) *The established and the outsiders*, edited by C. Wouters. Dublin: UCD Press.

Evans, B. and Bauman, Z. (2016) The refugee crisis is humanity's crisis, 2 May 2016, https://www.nytimes.com/2016/05/02/opinion/the-refugee-crisis-is-humanitys-crisis.html?_r=0

Foucault, M. (1965) *Madness and civilization*. London: Routledge.

Garreau, J. (1991) *Edge city: Life on the new frontier*. New York: Doubleday.

Kafka, F.(2009/1915) *Metamorphosis*. Eastford:Martino Fine Books.

Oxenham, M. (2013) *Higher education in liquid modernity*. London: Routledge.

Putnam, R. (2000) *Bowling alone: The collapse and revival of American community*. New York: Simon & Schuster.

Sartre, J. P. (1969) *Being and nothingness: An essay on phenomenological ontology*, trans. H. E. Barnes. London: Methuen.

Simmel, G. (1950/1908) The stranger. In K. Wolff (trans.), *The sociology of Georg Simmel* (pp. 402–408). New York: Free Press.

Turner, V. (1967) *The forest of symbols: Aspects of Ndembu Ritual*. Ithaca, NY: Cornell University Press.

Turner, V. (1969) *The ritual process: Structure and anti-structure*. Piscataway, NJ: Aldine Transaction.

Van Gennep, A. (1960/1908)*Rites of passage*. London: Routledge.

4

THE ASYLUM AND THE SELF

Erving Goffman on the stigma and the stranger

> While the stranger is present before us, evidence can arise of his possessing an attribute that makes him different from others in the category of persons available for him to be, and of a less desirable kind in the extreme, a person who is quite thoroughly bad, or dangerous, or weak.
>
> *(Goffman 1963: 12)*

Social life for Erving Goffman is identified as a product of inter-connected practices. A central concept within Goffman's approach to understanding social life is the *definition of the situation* or *frame*. This central idea is used to identify ordinary ways of behaving appropriately and ordinary ways of speaking appropriately that are embedded shared practical understandings of social life. It is for this reason that behaviours are often recurrent, becoming habitual when established over time. How people choose to 'behave in public places' (Goffman 1963) or to 'present themselves in everyday life' (Goffman 1959) involves the individual person drawing upon their personal motives, intentions and meanings in relation to the definition of the situation/frame, ritual or contextual factors. A key aspect of being a person is the ability to engage in the meaningful organisation of connectives; as meaningful interaction depends on connecting with others appropriately in the accepted manner. For Goffman, the pronoun, 'I' refers to a specific biographical entity, that is, more than the traditional sociological model of the individual as a person that is divided into multiple roles.

As we saw in Chapter 1 on Simmel, from Robert Park's concept of *Marginal Man*, through Paul Siu's concept of the *Sojourner*, Alfred Schütz's concept of the *Homecomer*, and Lewis Coser's understanding of the *Alien*, traditionally sociology has treated the stranger as a marginal figure, whose marginality can give rise to suspicion or hostility. In contrast, there are two interconnected conceptions of the stranger present in Goffman's work. First, the stranger is a person with whom we are co-present but not intimate with and we have no knowledge of their personal biography; as such we treat this person with a degree of 'civil inattention'. The second conception of the stranger in Goffman's work is an individual whose presence is not fully regarded as legitimate.

Civil inattention is given to a person who does 'normal' well or is effective at what Harvey Sacks (1984) calls 'doing being ordinary'. In his lecture 'On doing "being ordinary"', Sacks (1984) looks at the ways in which the individual constitutes themselves as 'ordinary' in any given situation: 'in effect, a job that persons and the people around them may be coordinatively engaged in, to achieve that each of them, together, are ordinary persons' (Sacks 1984: 415). The process also involves guidance in terms of what to look for in order to see how 'any scene you are in can be made an ordinary scene, a usual scene, and that is what that scene is' (Sacks 1984: 416). Individual people must work at and create the situation of 'nothing happened' by doing 'being ordinary' in any situation. People experience 'nothing happened' by 'being ordinary' as a set of constraints on experiences by achieving and presenting 'the ordinary cast of mind' (Sacks 1984: 424).

There is a custom of maintaining anonymity that governs behaviour in public between people who are co-present but who are not know to each other personally. In these circumstances people quickly glance at each other to make a judgement about the legitimacy of their presence, and then look away. This ritual underpins Goffman's conception of civil inattention; we acknowledge the presence of the other person but use the glance to communicate that we have no hostile intention but also that we are not seeking any sustained interaction. Civil inattention allows people to remain unknown to each other and maintain legitimate anonymity, a degree of strangeness. A safe and sound and accepted way of being in the world.

With Goffman's second conception of the stranger, where an individual's presence is not fully regarded as legitimate, the Other breaks the definition of the situation and consequently the Other is defined as a social type, the stranger. Co-participants make judgements about the individual whom they feel has departed from the definition of the situation and categorises the individual as a form or type of stranger. The stranger is seen as stigmatised, a category of unwanted, surplus and expendable 'Other'. Through this process of examining, the individual: 'is thus reduced in our minds from a whole and usual person to a tainted, discounted one' (Goffman 1963: 12).

In both cases strangeness is accomplished through practice. The definition of the situation is formed out of the situated activities of individual human agents and is the concept that Goffman uses to define practice as the link between agency and structure. However, as with other researchers who draw upon practice theory, Goffman's unit of analysis is not individual social actions, as he clearly states: 'the individual is not the natural unit for our consideration but rather the team and its members' (Goffman 1956: 93).

Presentation of self in everyday life

The dramaturgical approach that Goffman developed is derived from the approach to pragmatic philosophy developed by George Herbert Mead, William James and Charles Horton Cooley. The interactional element of Mead's conception of the social act has a significance on Goffman's analysis.

The social act for Mead is defined as the symbolisation of experience in which gesture, especially vocal gestures and other forms of communication, are directed towards other people. The actions of one person acts as an incentive for others co-present to respond in a socially appropriate way to the initial action. Considered or deliberate communication of gestures occurs when gestures become signs, that is when the individual making the gesture directs a definite meaning towards one or more individuals and expects that individual or individuals to respond in a predictable and appropriate manner. The subsequent behaviour of the people present involves the mutual adjustment towards one another. The social act generates the expectation of an adjustive response from the others present based upon the reading and interpretation of the gesture. Implicit within the social act are three basic distinct components: 'namely, in the triadic relation of a gesture of one individual, a response to that gesture by a second individual, and completion of the given social act initiated by the gesture of the first individual' (Mead 1962/1934: 81).

The content of mind and the development of self stand in relation to this triadic relation of gesture within the social act; as it is within this triadic relation that the social process upon which the understanding of meaning in a situation is developed. There are two general stages in the development of the self for Mead; in the first stage:

> the individual's self is constituted simply by an organization of the particular attitudes of other individuals toward himself and toward one another in the specific social acts ... [in the second stage] self is constituted not only by an organization of these particular individual attitudes, but also by an organization of the social attitudes of the generalized other or the social group as a whole to which he belongs.
>
> *(Mead 1962/1934: 158)*

Mead's conception of self is then a 'process' rather than a 'substance' constructed out of a:

> conversation of gestures [that] has been internalized within an organic form. This process does not exist for itself, but is simply a phase of the whole social organization of which the individual is a part. The organization of the social act has been imported into the organism and becomes then the mind of the individual.
>
> *(Mead 1962/1934: 178)*

This process of relating to the Other by a conversation of internalised gestures becomes central to the conduct of the individual and underlies the development of the 'I' and the 'me' that underpins Mead's construction of self (Mead 1962/1934: 179). 'I' is the subjective and unreflective aspect of self that contains those elements of self that make us unique individuals. In contrast the 'Me' is our 'object self', the self that we reflect upon and edit with reference to the potential responses of others, before presenting ourselves in everyday life and engaging in interaction. The I and the Me are the concepts developed by Mead to describe the ability of an individual to conceive of themselves as both a subject and an object. Shared gestures facilitate organised forms of social activity, allowing individual members to act in a manner that is 'social' by identifying the attitudes of others and incorporating those attitudes into their motives and intention to action:

> A social act may be defined as one in which the occasion or sti- mulus which sets free an impulse is found in the character or conduct of a living form that belongs to the proper environment of the living form whose impulse it is. I wish, however, to restrict the social act to the claw of acts which involve the co-operation of more than one individual, and whose object as defined by the act, in the sense of Bergson, is a social object. I mean by a social object one that answers to all the parts of the complex act, though these parts are found in the conduct of different individuals. The objec- tive of the acts is then found in the life-process of the group, not in those of the separate individuals alone.
>
> *(Mead 1925: 263–264)*

Different elements of the social act are created and presented by indi- viduals to the others who are co-present and if these elements appear in the acts of each other individual this can act as a stimulus for the others present to further respond. Goffman builds upon this observation and suggests that when a person comes into the presence of others, that person is commonly assessed by those present in terms of a whole range of personal qualities such as their socio-economic status, attitude toward the other present, their honesty, etc. Both the individual and the people present project a 'definition of the situation' that forms a contribution to an emerging mutual understanding about the relationship between self and Other. The definition of the situation forms: 'a surface of agreement, this veneer of consensus, is facilitated by each participant concealing his own wants behind statements which assert values to which everyone present is likely to give lip-service' (Goffman 1956: 4). The projected definition of the situation has a distinctive moral character for Goffman, in that one of the organising principles of social life is that: 'any individual who possesses certain social characteristics has a moral right to expect that others will value and treat him in a correspondingly appropriate way' (Goffman 1956: 6). When a person enters a situation, we ask ourselves if they are 'authorised' to perform in the ways that they do, or if they are engaged in some form of impersonation or deception, either misrepresenting themselves as individuals or misrepresenting the category of people to whom they claim to belong (Goffman 1956: 39). *Realness* is achieved within a situation when an individual chooses the appropriate way of behaving in a given 'setting' in the opinion of the others present. Such a person demonstrates that they have the appropriate 'appearance' and 'manner' to legitimately claim to have the moral character that they present. Goffman calls this performance 'personal front'.

The presentation of *front* tends to become institutionalised as a set of abstract stereotyped expectations, which give meaning and stability to our social identity. The front becomes a 'collective representation' and such fronts tend to be selected rather than created (Goffman 1956: 17). When describing a successful performance of a front, Goffman describes the successful performer as a *practitioner* (Goffman 1956: 23). The personal front will change over time. Fashions in relation to presentation of self that were considered fashionable at one time may fall out of style later and a person may feel the need to change the way they present themselves in everyday life.

Challenging the legitimacy of a personal front is not something that people treat lightly, Goffman agrees with Durkheim's argument: 'The human personality is a sacred thing; one does not violate it nor infringe its bounds, while at the same time the greatest good is in communion with others' (Durkheim 1953: 37 cited in Goffman 1956: 46).

Goffman explains the process of selecting the appropriate front for a given situation, in a manner that has much in common with Simmel's conception of the third, Mead's generalised Other and Cooley's looking glass self. In Mead's analysis the self has no meaning outside of society, in that the self only has meaning in response to the generalised Other. Similarly, for Cooley the self is reflected in what he named the reflexive self or the looking-glass self; our self-conception arises from the impressions we get about ourselves based upon what we can gather about others' interpretations of us. Goffman also presents a view that our social identity is based upon the way we successfully or unsuccessfully present ourselves in everyday life:

> When a performer guides his private activity in accordance with incorporated moral standards, he may associate these standards with a reference group of some kind so that, in a sense, there will be a non-present audience for his activity. This possibility leads us to consider a further one. The individual may privately maintain standards of behaviour which he does not personally believe in, maintaining these standards because of a lively belief that an unseen audience is present which will punish deviations from these standards. In other words, an individual may be his own audience or may imagine an audience to be present.
>
> *(Goffman 1956: 50)*

Goffman goes on to explain that successful performances are the ones that are supported by like-minded people, a team of similar performers who cooperate with each other in presentation of a performance; what Goffman calls 'dramaturgical co-operation' (Goffman 1956: 51), these individuals become dependent upon each other in the successful maintenance of a definition of the situation. When people share a common feeling of agreement what they share feels real and solid and provides a sense of security:

> A team, then, may be defined as a set of individuals whose intimate co-operation is required if a given projected definition of the situation is to be maintained. A team is a grouping, but it is a grouping not in relation to a social structure or social organization but rather in relation to an interaction or series of interactions in which the relevant definition of the situation is maintained.
>
> *(Goffman 1956: 66)*

Social life also takes place within what Goffman describes as 'regions'. Within a region people have a perception that there are barriers that are bounded by perception. There is the 'back region' where performances are devised, and favoured impressions chosen, costumes selected and personal front scrutinised and adjusted. Front region is where the managed impression is performed in the presence of others. However, there is a third region that Goffman identifies as 'the outside'. The outside is neither part of the front region nor the back region and the people who are from the outside are the strangers. If a stranger were to unexpectedly enter either the front or the back region this would disrupt the performance or the preparation of the performance (Goffman 1956: 82–83).

Front regions and back regions are constructed and defined in relation to the presence of a potential stranger using what Goffman refers to as 'protective practices'. These practices are 'defence techniques' and are politically, culturally and/or value driven. The 'defensive practices' are established for controlling access to the back and front region and include: loyalty, discipline and circumspection (Goffman 1956: 146, 153).

The presence of the stranger can make team members question the definition of the situation, disrupt the perceived *realness* of the situation and undermine the feeling of security. The stranger is not a team member and does not share the definition of the situation and has no vested interest in maintaining the team's bounded perception of themselves. The presence of the stranger makes impression management more difficult to achieve as the stranger is viewed as an individual who has seen a performance that was not for their eyes. In social life, explains Goffman: 'We specialise … in keeping strangers out, and in giving the performer some privacy in which to prepare himself for the show' (Goffman 1956: 157). Strangers often find themselves treated as if they are not present. The definition of the situation is maintained by the effective use of power as a mechanism of exclusion including naked power such as physical coercion, the use of persuasion or the withdrawal of civil inattention:

> It may also be added that a team can treat an individual as if he were not present, doing this not because it is the natural thing or the only feasible thing to do, but as a pointed way of expressing

hostility to an individual who has conducted himself improperly. In such situations, the important show is to show the outcast that he is being ignored, and the activity that is carried on in order to demonstrate this.

(Goffman 1956: 96)

In *Behaviour in Public Places*, Goffman (1962: 216) developed the argument that improper conduct in one situation can indicate a general disenfranchisement of self in other face-to-face interaction. In other words, when an individual intentionally or unintentionally conducts themselves in a way that others consider situationally improper, the person is either alienated from, or an alien to, the gathering. In addition, the situational impropriety can also provide other information about the person's condition and about the person's wider relationships in social life.

Any situationally offensive act can be conducted either voluntarily or involuntarily. Situational improprieties can also be used as a means of expressing resentment towards an individual or group. The people who witness the offensive act will ask: Is the person aware of the implications of the acts and chose to perform them with these implications in mind? Co-participants must decide on the degree of intentionality. Did the person have extenuating reasons for behaving in the way that they did? Is the offensive behaviour because the individual: 'is accustomed to a different idiom and structure of involvement from the ones sanctioned by those in the situation' (Goffman 1963: 219). Is the offensive act one that the individual can control and as such the person might be willing to alter their conduct if they were to appreciate its significance? If the person unaware of the situational obligations? Or, is the behaviour a gesture of contempt for the gathering?

One way of correcting situational offenses is to look upon the offender as someone who is unnatural, who is not quite a human being, for then the offense becomes a reflection on him and not on what he has offended.

(Goffman 1963: 235)

What is 'the definition of the situation'?

In any situation individuals may find themselves searching for the meaning of the events and ask themselves or others around them: What is going on here? The definition of the situation is the social world of everyday life that people who share a common culture can recognise. We experience the definition of the situation as a set of moral demands or practical constraints upon us as individuals in terms of setting parameters to what we can do in a given situation; the legitimate way of being in the world. The definition of the situation is then not solely subjectively constructed by the individual. Individuals can contribute to it, individuals can choose to ignore it, but it is not an individual creation. The definition of the situation is the mechanism that allows us to think of the world as socially organised. Conceptually the definition of the situation has much in common with Alfred Schutz's understanding of 'the natural attitude', which is based upon the assumption that 'the world out there' is presupposed in that it has a 'given' or taken for granted quality that people acknowledge in their choice of actions. The definition of the situation 'frames' the social action taking place. Without some form of framework to define what is going on within any situation, social life would be meaningless. Goffman's understanding of 'definition of the situation' is focused on the structure of experience and contains within it a conception of practice that is more fully and systematically explored with his later concept of 'frame'. As Karl Scheibe suggests: 'human beings seem incapable of regarding any social situation as not having some sort of frame, and that every frame is a manifestation of tacit piety' (Scheibe 2002: 200).

The concept of the definition of the situation was first used in the social sciences by W. I. Thomas, who famously stated: 'If men define situations as real, they are real in their consequences.' However, Thomas also added the insight that, 'There is always a rivalry between the spontaneous definitions of the situation made by the member of an organized society and the definitions which his society has provided for him' (Thomas 1923: 42).

For Goffman, sociologists had largely ignored the second part of Thomas's account of the concept:

> At present, the idea of the social situation is handled in the most happy-go-lucky way .... I do not think this opportunistic approach to social situations is always valid. It can be argued that social situations, at least in our society, constitute a reality sui generis, as he used to say and, therefore, need and warrant analysis in their own right, much like that accorded other basic forms of social organization.
>
> *(Goffman 1964: 133)*

Thomas suggests there are two aspects of the definition of the situation: the subjective motivation of the human agent and the external objective constraint of society found in culture and values. One of the central themes in Goffman's early career was to bring together the two aspects of Thomas's conception to explain how meaning is established within a situation. The definition of the situation was to be a central concept within Goffman's misunderstood dramaturgical approach. The two related conceptions of the stranger in Goffman's work are linked by Mead's conception of the 'social act':

> The social process relates the responses of one individual to the gestures of another, as the meanings of the latter, and is thus responsible for the rise of and existence of new objects in the social situation, objects depending upon or constituted by these meanings. Meaning is thus not to be conceived fundamentally as a state of consciousness or as a set of organized relations existing or subsisting mentally outside the field of experience into which they enter; on the contrary, it should be conceived objectively as having its existence entirely within the field itself. The response of one organism to the gesture of another in any given social act is the meaning of that gesture.
>
> *(Mead 1962: 78)*

Human agency is the only entity capable of creating and establishing meaning, but agents must co-exist with other human agents who also possess the ability to create and establish meaning. Although we can never fully understand the knowledge that other people have inside their heads, or the subjective experiences of the people with whom we are co-present with have about us and the situation we are sharing, we assume that other people have an understanding and knowledge of the situation and that part of this understanding may be highly subjective and personal. We also know that understanding and knowledge, including those aspects that are highly subjective and personal, are part of the constitution of the self of the people who are co-present. In addition, we know that no situated action is without social or communicative content, but it can be misunderstood. People have the ability to read and interpret both the spoken word of the other people who are co-present and their gestures. The definition of the situation is a co-creation between the individuals within the situation, but some people are more skilled at imposing their view of the content of the definition of the situation and at undermining agents who may attempt to redefine the meaning, shape and form of the action.

Although Goffman's approach to social life is commonly described as dramaturgical, social reality is not 'like a play' for Goffman. However, Goffman did assume that people do have a dramatistic ontology, in that people with whom we are co-present feel the need to know whom we are, and whom are the other people that are also co-present. In addition, people like to have a clear understanding of what their role is in the situation and the intentions of the co-present individuals. For Goffman, to present a preferred definition of the situation is to dramatize it, by which Goffman means to 'stage' our preferred definition of the situation. There is a conceptual connection between the behaviour we observe in others, our own skills and abilities to define what is ontologically secure about the situation and to convince others that our interpretation is correct. The definition of the situation is an achievement, a product of positioning and responding about the extent to which actions are socially acceptable to all the people present. Again, there is a link with Mead's conception of the social act:

> The response of one organism to the gesture of another in any given social act is the meaning of that gesture and is also in a sense responsible for the appearance or coming into being of the new object-or a new content of an old object-to which that gesture refers through the outcome of the given social act.

> (Mead 1964: 78)

To avoid misunderstanding, when people are in each other's company everyone must take steps to ensure that all people present have a clear understanding of each other's motives and intentions. Civil inattention is central to the presentation of a legitimate self within the situation. In *Frame Analysis* Goffman (1974) spells out his understanding of the ontological status of the definition of the situation:

> Defining situations as real certainly has consequences, but these may contribute very marginally to the events in progress; in some cases only a slight embarrassment flits across the scene in mild concern for those who tried to define the situation wrongly. All the world is not a stage – certainly theatre isn't entirely. (Whether you organize a theatre or an aircraft factory, you need to find places for cars to park and coats to be checked, and these had better be real places, which, incidentally, had better carry real insurance against theft.) Presumably, a 'definition of the situation' is almost always to be found, but those who are in the situation do not create this definition, even though their society can be said to do so; ordinarily, all they do is to assess correctly what the situation ought to be for them and then act accordingly. True, we personally negotiate aspects of all these arrangements under which we live, but often once these are negotiated, we continue on mechanically, as though the matter had always been settled. So, too, there are occasions when we must wait until are almost over before discovering what has been occurring, and occasions of our own activity when we can considerably put off deciding what to claim we have been doing. But surely these are not the only principles of organization. Social life is dubious enough and ludicrous enough without having to wish it further into unreality.
>
> *(Goffman 1974: 1–2)*

Goffman goes on to make a distinction between 'role' and 'character': individuals can perform a variety of social roles in many situations and underpinning each role is the same character or individual personality. An individual is only allowed a voice within a situation if they adopt an acceptable role. If people who are co-present question the performance of the role, they may also question the underpinning character of the individual performing the role, making a connection between the person's character and the mis-framing of the situation. Alternatively, people may have differing or contradictory understandings of the definition of the situation; making the definition fragile, ambiguous, subject to dispute or otherwise uncertain, and as such the definition can become discredited, although the individuals involved in that situation may not be subjected to becoming defined as discredited people. When an individual is in the circumstances of not understanding the situation, or feels that they are in doubt or error, they very quickly attempt to reach an understanding of the situation.

In such circumstances frame disputes are possible; although most of the time our interpretative frameworks are adequate for the situation, there are always vulnerabilities to the framing process and in our interpretation and organisation of our own experience. In addition, individuals can attempt to generate a negative experience for others by encouraging them to adopt incorrect assumptions about the situation, causing them embarrassment when they articulate a false or incorrect interpretation.

In *Frame Analysis*, Goffman (1974) refers to William James' (1950/ 1869) question: Under what circumstances do we think things are real? He also refers to Gregory Bateson (1972), in *A Theory of Play and Phantasy*, and Alfred Schutz (1962/1945), with their conceptions of the conditions that must be fulfilled to accept something as 'real'. Goffman makes clear that those individuals who are in the definition of the situation do not necessarily create the definition, they simply assume that a shared understanding or set of practices has been established. Within organisations a definition of the situation or frame can have a protected identity (Goffman 1974: 499) in that it is so well entrenched in institutional practices that it becomes difficult for participants to re-frame or manipulate the definition. However, in the last analysis, individuals are still active participants within the definition of the situation in that they must personally come to a correct understanding of it and behave appropriately.

Like Bateson (1972), Goffman looks at frame as a contextual device, formed out of habit that makes understanding of the situation possible. Habit is learned by the person, and the person is viewed by Goffman as a 'live agent' (Goffman 1974: 22) who has the ability to abstract what is meaningful from habit and transfer this abstracted meaning to other similar situations as a potentially suitable reading of the definition of the new situation.

Practice, or 'framing practices' (Goffman 1974: 246) are described by Goffman as the 'guided doings' of human agents within a situation. Practice transforms activity into a keying and a key can only translate what is already meaningful into a primary framework (Goffman 1974: 81). A key is a set of conventions by which a given activity is identified as containing a pattern that allows an unambiguous reading or understanding of the activity. Keying, the process of one or more individuals suggesting the appropriate key for an activity, allows for fabrication of meaning of the activity, intentionally managing an activity in such a way as to suggest to those present that actions observed is one thing when it is really another. All face to face interaction takes place reflexively and we need to be aware that a change in the definition of the situation may be required at any time.

Individuals always have some understanding of what Goffman calls the 'information state'; some knowledge of how and why events present themselves as they do, the forces that underpin the events and the intents of the people who are driving the events. An important structural feature of framed activities is tracking; the track is the story line or plot of any activity:

> facial features are the evidential boundary he employs during face-to-face interaction. Except, then, for leakage due to involuntary emotional expression, the actor is able (and often willing) to play an information game, selectively withholding from interrogators what they would like to know.
>
> *(Goffman 1974: 513)*

The evidential boundary of a frame is established by convention, which Goffman describes as the primary social framework, or by physical barriers, which Goffman describes as the primary natural framework (Goffman 1974: 232). Goffman explains that the central difference between natural and social frameworks is the central role of agency within the social framework. Within the natural framework individuals are subjected to a 'deterministic, will less, nonmoral way of being'

(Goffman 1974: 188). The individual is a 'guided object, not a guiding agent' (Goffman 1974: 189). In the social framework the individual is viewed as a human agent with moral and legal responsibility for their actions. The individual is assumed to be competent and to have control over their intentions.

When co-present individuals make a judgement about the competence of an individual, a judgement must be made of whether their incapacities are personal failings or institutionally sustained. Co-present individuals also need to decide on the degree of non-responsibility that should be given to the individual. The stranger is 'out of the frame', by which Goffman means that they are beyond the evidential boundary of our understanding. The evidential boundary of a frame is then established by convention or by physical barriers (Goffman 1974: 232). However, not all individuals within a situation have full 'participation status' (Goffman 1974: 224). Some people are treated as 'within the frame' but do not have the full status of participants because of: a perceived or assumed difference; a lack of continuity of their role performance; a performance that deviates from the script that may indicate the person belongs to another frame; or they are assumed to be making use of an out of frame channel to gain an advantage over the people who are co-present.

The frame is the intersection between the individual motive and intention and the external practice (Goffman 1974: 249). Frames construct a boundary and social activity is bounded but the brackets that bind the activity are not in themselves part of the action but markers that frame or identify 'the natural boundaries of episodes of activity' (Goffman 1974: 251) that 'practitioners' (Goffman 1974: 252) make use of in any situation. Goffman gives the example of the use of the gavel in the courtroom. It is not part of the action but helps to establish the beginning or end of an activity. Bracketing becomes more important to sustaining action when the definition of the situation is fragile. However, when an individual breaks from the frame they become 'interactionally disorganised' or they have to successfully shift key. The unsuccessful shifting of key can be the trigger that causes an individual to become defined as strange. Connectives are devices within an interpretative activity that allow individuals to draw upon experience to shape the definition of the situation, they help to situate who is doing what and saying what in a situation (Goffman 1974: 537).

The frame structure of talk and the frame structure of the theatre have much in common, Goffman suggests. However, in the context of the theatre the people who are co-present know that the action presented is scripted and 'not real'. With everyday interaction the question is one of how real what is presented by the individuals is in any situation. Practice transforms activity into keying and a key can only translate what is already meaningful into a primary framework (Goffman 1974: 78, 81) Keying also allows for fabrication of activity, intentionally managing an activity, suggesting to those present that it is one thing when it is really another. All face-to-face interaction takes place reflexively and we need to be aware that a change in the definition of the situation may be required at any time.

When it comes to attempts to categorise the Other as 'stranger', people attempt to do this by the creation of 'pejorative constructions' within the definition of the situation, as Berger and Luckmann (1966: 72) explain: 'Reciprocal typifications of actions are built up in the course of a shared history. They cannot be created instantaneously', however it is not uncommon for individuals attempt to 'control human conduct by setting up predefined patterns of conduct, which channel it in one direction as against the many other directions that would theoretically be possible'.

People live in a world of face-to-face and mediated social encounters. Within such encounters people feel an obligation to 'show a face'; to act in a way that expresses their understanding of the situation. Face is defined by Goffman as the positive value that an individual claims to have within the situation and the judgement we make of the face of the others who are present. Although we act as if the face is our own personal possession, as it can provide a sense of security and pleasure, the face is a 'social' face in that it can be taken away from the person if they do not live up to the definition of the situation. The social occasion is based upon a behavioural order, which is 'found in all peopled places' (Goffman 1967: 2) and itself is composed of 'countless patterns and natural sequences of behaviour occurring whenever persons come into contact with one another's immediate presence' (Goffman 1967: 2).

These patterns are described by Goffman as a 'normatively stabilized structure' (Goffman 1967: 2).

Goffman's conception of a 'normatively stabilized structure' is based
upon a code or rules of social interaction. The presence of the code
does not determine behaviour within an encounter, in that it does not
explain why a person has chosen to enter an encounter. We choose to
enter an encounter but once the choice of encounter has been made
there are expectations about how to present one's self and how to
behave. Goffman describes these expectations as a 'repertoire of face-
saving practices" (Goffman 1967: 13) rooted in the 'perceptiveness' of
the individuals within a social encounter. Maintaining a face within a
definition of the situation is what Goffman terms 'face-work'; defensive
and protective practices for the maintenance of self (Goffman 1967: 14).
Practice in this sense is a ritual code within face-work that people must
be skilled in to avoid departing from the definition of the situation:
'whenever the physical possibility of spoken interaction arises, it seems
that a system of practices, conventions, and procedural rules comes into
play which functions as a means of guiding and organizing the flow of
messages' (Goffman 1967: 34).

Practice guides but does not determine behaviour within an
encounter. Individuals who refuse to accept the definition of the
situation can arouse anxiety amongst those people who do accept it.
The stranger is an individual who is not 'practised' in the face-work
required within a definition of the situation, the stranger does not
appear to feel as others feel and does not appear to know that their
acts are causing offence or injury. Strangers are individuals who are
often thrust into interactions that they did not choose or expect, they
often experience a feeling of 'ritual disequilibrium' when faced with
an unfamiliar definition of the situation, which makes them: 'danger-
ously dependent upon the cooperative forbearance of the others'
(Goffman 1967: 18). Others who are present in the social encounter
with the stranger can choose how to respond to the inability of the
stranger to read and respond to the definition of the situation and
options vary from patience, restraint and tolerance to annoyance,
irritation and hostility. The others must move forward in the interaction with the stranger, by attempting to make the behaviours of the
stranger understandable, perhaps looking for extenuating circumstances

or viewing the actions an unintentional or alternatively viewing the actions as a threat. The latter option occurs when the stranger appears to refuse to accept the definition of the situation and continues to engage in offending behaviour. The stranger can always find themselves excluded, or in Goffman's terms denied the status of an 'interactant' in our encounters (Goffman 1967: 14).

When a person begins an encounter they already have some form of social relationship or understanding of co-participation with the others present. This is reflected in ceremonies of greeting and farewell. The role of the greeting is to define or clarify the roles that each of the participants will take during the interaction. The stranger comes to be regarded as *the third* in Goffman's analysis of face-work. The third is the individual interactant who is assumed to hold the view of the generalised Other or the public. The presence of a third can be disruptive to the co-participation underpinning the social relationship: 'Furthermore, in many relationships, the members come to share a face, so that in the presence of third parties an improper act on the part of one member becomes a source of acute embarrassment to the other members' (Goffman 1967: 42).

In summary, social encounters are only possible for Goffman if co-participants can mobilise each other to act as self-regulating participants. One way of mobilising the individual is through ritual. A social encounter is a 'ritually organized system of social activity' (Goffman 1967: 45). Ritual is of 'practical use' for the interactant to become a co-participant and we draw upon practices to maintain a specified ritual equilibrium (Goffman 1967: 45). The rituals and practices that people draw upon within the definition of the situation act as a mechanism of exclusion. The person who breaks the definition of the situation is excluded but still physically present and visible and remains in a relationship, albeit redefined, with the people co-present. This situation of the individual being present but redefined in negative terms does not only apply to the moral career of the mental patient but is central to the construction of marginalisation, the taking away of full rights to participation and the creation of an exclusionary order that applies to wider populations. Institutional racism for example is one such form of exclusionary order created and maintained in this way.

Moral career and the process of estrangement

The term 'career' is usually understood as the process of entry and progression within a respectable professional occupation. Goffman (1961) uses the term 'moral career' in a broader sense to refer to the processes of becoming by which an individual develops to attain a legitimate position as a member of a social category or type of person. For Goffman a moral career is composed of the 'progressive changes that occur in the beliefs that he has concerning himself and significant others' (Goffman 1961: 14). The moral career comes to shape the individual's sense of their social self and their felt identity.

When individuals enters a total institution such as a locked ward in a mental hospital they do so with a conception of themselves created by reference to 'stable social arrangements' drawn from their social and family life. When entering the total institution, through the process of hospitalization, individuals lose that social support provided previously in their social life. They experience a deconstruction of their 'civilian selves' by the imposition of 'rituals of degradation', a series of 'abasements, degradations, humiliations, and profanations of self' by which the self is 'systematically, if often unintentionally, mortified' (Goffman 1961: 14). This process brings about a feeling of depersonalisation or a curtailment of the individual's previous self.

Goffman is keen to point out that: 'that perception of losing one's mind is based on culturally derived and socially engrained stereotypes as to the significance of symptoms such as hearing voices, losing temporal and spatial orientation, and sensing that one is being followed' (Goffman 1961: 132).

In terms of mental patients, most report that their moral career began with a complaint about some aspect of their behaviour in a public place. For this reason, Goffman views the moral career a process of re-socialisation that has a social rather than psychological origin. The term 'career contingencies' applies to the degree to which the situational impropriety was visible, subjected to the harsh and judgmental gaze of others and the degree of response from the other individuals who were co-present. The transition from person to patient is the fundamental transition in the moral career of the mental patient. However, each stage in the career process is rooted in continuous moral review that brings with it a redefinition of the position of the person from their role of pre-patient, through a consequent loss of freedom, separation from civil society and undermining of self. There is communal reconstruction and imposition of a category of social identity rooted in a perception of personal failure and the person is labelled as undeserving, leading to an increasing separation from all aspects of their previous life; a condition and set of circumstances that the pre-patient did not want or invite.

There is then for Goffman always a 'social beginning' to the patient's moral career; some form of complaint is made against the individual about their behaviour, which eventually leads to hospitalisation. Career contingencies are then central for Goffman to the actions of individual human agents or organisations that facilitate or mediate an individual's passage from civilian to patient status. Outside of a context of mental illness and hospitalisation, the actions of individual human agents or organisations facilitate and mediate the individual's passage along a given moral career and transition to a stigmatised status. Examples that Goffman cites include: a man's psychotic behaviour is tolerated by his partner until she meets a new boyfriend, and 'a rebellious adolescent daughter can no longer be managed at home because she now threatens to have an open affair with an unsuitable companion' (Goffman 1961: 135). In Goffman's view, many mental patients do not suffer from mental illness, but from the 'contingencies' of their unacceptable behaviours and this is also true for stigmatised statuses not connected with mental illness and hospitalisation. The inability to protect one's self from the contingencies of having a category imposed upon one's self often involves the categorised individual having to come to terms with the fact that their behaviour is unacceptable to others; this constitutes a 'moral' experience for Goffman that further separates the labelled individual from the people who have applied the label:

> in casting off the raiment of the old self – or in having the cover torn away – the person need not seek a new robe and a new audience before which to cower. Instead he can learn, at least for a time, to practice before all groups the amoral arts of shamelessness.
> *(Goffman 1961: 169)*

Goffman (1961) explains that underpinning each moral career is an institutional set of arrangements for the regulation of self:

> The self is not a property of the person to whom it is attributed, but dwells rather in the pattern of social control that is exerted in connection with the person by himself and those around him. This special kind of institutional arrangement does not so much support the self as constitute it.
>
> *(Goffman 1961: 168)*

All individuals have a 'self-story' that is incorporated into their sense of personal identity, but the self-story of the stranger is usually ignored by communities of people who regard each other as not strangers unless that story can be incorporated into the imposition of the preferred social identity that the stranger has now come to be recognised by. Goffman's work is not directly concerned with the characteristics of Western legal and political systems. However, if we generalise Goffman's conception of the moral career beyond Goffman's discussion of the mental hospital as a total institution, Goffman is describing the mechanisms for a carceral society. The moral career has a guilt-carrying function that is essentially embedded in a process of inferiorisation, underpinned by the threat of involuntary confinement. For Goffman the individual who is perceived to create or cause a situational impropriety will be perceived to be carrying a stigma and is likely to be identified as a category of stranger. Any person can perform a situational impropriety that can be labelled as falling foul of the accepted ways of behaving within a culture and this is the starting point for exclusion from the wider society, the start of a moral career and entry into a form of total institution. There are several similarities between Foucault's and Goffman's understanding of the mechanisms of power. Both Foucault and Goffman give a central place to the gaze in maintaining power. Both view solidarity as essentially groundless in that it requires practices and rituals to give it cohesion. In addition, inevitably with solidarity come forms of exclusion; individuals and groups who are not us and against whom we measure ourselves run the risk of exclusion. For both Foucault and Goffman all of us are potentially excludable. Moreover, the central role of control and domination that Foucault describes as the bio-political function of Western law and politics has much in common with the regulation of behaviour via career contingencies in Goffman's account of the moral career. In *The*

Use of Pleasure, for example, Foucault has a focus on subjectification, which has much in common with Goffman's account of self-work/ face-work in that: 'one performs on oneself, not only in order to bring one's conduct into compliance with a given rule, but to attempt to transform oneself into the ethical subject of one's behaviour' (Foucault 1990/1984: 27).

The meaning and significance of the moral career in the construction of self, felt identity, social identity and stigma cannot be overstated. Outside of the discussion of the moral career on the mental patient Goffman explains that:

> Each moral career, and behind this, each self, occurs within the confines of an institutional system, whether a social establishment such as a mental hospital or a complex of personal and professional relationships. The self, then, can be seen as something that resides in the arrangements prevailing in a social system for its members. The self in this sense is not a property of the person to whom it is attributed, but dwells rather in the pattern of social control that is exerted in connection with the person by himself and those around him. This special kind of institutional arrangement does not so much support the self as constitute it.
>
> *(Goffman 1961: 168)*

The stranger and the stigmatised

> [S]tigma – the situation of the individual who is disqualified from full social acceptance.
>
> *(Goffman 1963a: preface)*

Appearance is a form of communication by which a person announces their preferred identity. Stigmatised individuals are regarded as 'misfits' (Garland-Thomson 2011, Price 2015). Goffman (1964) explains that, within face-to-face engagements, cultural rules establish how individuals should appropriately conduct themselves within the gathering. Part of the appropriate way of behaving is presenting an image of self that reflects the facts of their situation and the role they perform with those who are co-present. Within the definition of the situation the individual can become aware, or can be made aware, of an actual or potential discrepancy between their 'real' and 'projected' selves. Goffman (1962) develops the concept of 'cooling the mark out' as an aspect of the definition of the situation when an individual's attempt at 'management of the scene' is unsuccessful, most notably when a person constructs a conception of themselves for which they do not have the resources to sustain. The person cannot maintain the public claim to be defined in a way and consequently they are examined and then doubted before being subjected to an 'involuntary loss of role'. It is not uncommon for people to want to protect themselves when the facts of their status do not support the position they claim to have. To be involuntarily deprived of a role can reflect unfavourably, as such the condition of being 'cooled out' can lead to embarrassment:

> Any event which demonstrates that someone has made a false claim, defining himself as something which he is not, tends to destroy him. If others realize that the person's conception of self has been contradicted and discredited, then the person tends to be destroyed in the eyes of others. If the person can keep the contradiction a secret, he may succeed in keeping everyone but himself from treating him as a failure.
>
> *(Goffman 1962: 500)*

An understanding of the definition of the situation allows an individual to conduct him- or herself comfortably in interaction. Embarrassment is a deviation from the normal state of ease that we find in everyday interaction. Embarrassment disrupts the smooth running of interactions that sustain encounters; as such, when embarrassment is present ordinary involvement in the interaction will come to an end. For Goffman, any social encounter has the risk of becoming embarrassing for one or more of the people co-present. Any offence against propriety can lead to embarrassment. Embarrassment has an important social purpose, as the discomfort of embarrassment acts as a sanction that can be imposed upon people who unsuccessfully attempt to project a false or incomplete definition of themselves. Embarrassment is not an irrational impulse that disrupts the normal ways of behaving within a definition of the situation, rather embarrassment is a socially prescribed mechanism of response following permitting conflict and should be understood as an aspect of orderly behaviour; most notably when one or more legitimate organisational principles upon which a self draws upon to build their identity are questioned:

> By the standards of the wider society, perhaps only the discredited individual ought to feel ashamed; but, by the standards of the little social system maintained through the interaction, the discreditor is just as guilty as the person he discredits – sometimes more so, for, if he has been posing as a tactful man, in destroying another's image he destroys his own.
>
> *(Goffman 1956a: 268)*

In Goffman's analysis, 'identity norms' reproduce deviance as well as conformance. The process of attempting to identify a discrepancy and the assessment of personal qualities are referred to by Goffman as 'profiling'. Goffman uses the term 'cognitive recognition' to refer to the perceptual act of 'placing' an individual into a category. The allocation of attributes allows people co-present to stigmatize or confirm the usualness of a person. Stigma is for Goffman the identification of an 'undesired differentness' from what people who are co-present had anticipated (Goffman 1963a: 5). Broadly Goffman identifies three different types of stigma, all of which come to contaminate a person's social identity and can lead to nonacceptance: abominations of the body composed of various physical deformities or physical disability; blemishes of individual character such as individuals who are perceived as weak willed, domineering or unable to control unnatural passions, such as rigid beliefs or dishonesty; and finally the tribal stigma of race, nation and religion (Goffman 1963a: 4).

Individuals who have a stigma in common tend to have similar life experiences and share a similar 'moral career'. One aspect of the moral career is that the stigmatised person comes to understands the standpoint of the normal, the shared beliefs about the stigma that are common in the wider society and the consequences of possessing the stigma. The individual who for whatever reason cannot maintain an identity norm will find themselves categorised as a person with little value. *Difference* may become defined as an inferior or shameful form of difference and the basis for a stigmatised identity, a: 'precarious self, subject to abuse and discrediting' (Goffman 1963a: 135).

The concept of stigma raises more questions than it facilitates answers as individuals can resist the application of a stigma. As stigma involves a deviation from the definition of the situation it is always associated within identifying the Other as a person who has exhibited personal errors and moral or ethical failures. Interdependency is a necessary aspect of our humanness and when interdependency is removed this can be experienced by the individual as a form of aloneness, oppression and subordination. The creation and imposition of aloneness are a central aspect of social exclusion and have a negative impact on our sense of self. However, a wide range of groups have successfully appropriated terms of abuse and used them to promote a positive identity, for example the term 'crip': an attempt to politically reclaim the historically derogatory term 'cripple', and the term 'queer' to undermine discrimination on grounds of sexuality.

Tribal stigma: race, nation and religion

Stigma, human mobility and migration have been interconnected for many years in both political debates and academic research, particularly so since the post-2015 'migration crisis' when there was a noticeable rise in the numbers of people seeking asylum in Europe. The conflict in Syria had displaced an estimated 4.9 million people by 2017 (UNHCR, 2017). The UNHCR (2015) estimated that by 2015 one in every 122 people in the world were seeking refuge in a place that was not their home. However, Lafleur and Mescoli (2018) argue that restrictions on the 'mobility of the poor' is also a European Union wide phenomenon that goes beyond specific national and ethnic groups in Europe. Politicians across the EU have drawn upon the concept of 'welfare tourism' to question the right of EU migrants to claim social assistance when they cross EU borders.

Stigma is part of the discourse that shapes EU migrants' experiences, even when those migrants are exercising their right to labour mobility. Directive 2004/38 on the right of citizens of the Union to exercise free movement of labour restricted the movement of citizens from new EU members from Southern, Central and Eastern Europe, as the older EU member states feared an influx of poor EU migrants. With a focus on EU migrants from Southern, Central and Eastern Europe, Lafleur and Mescoli (2018: 492) argue that: 'European legislation that allows national authorities to remove the residence permits of poor migrants accused of being burdens on the welfare state has been used to limit their freedom of movement'. Such 'burdens' include people who are long-term sick, unemployed and other 'unproductive migrants'. Roma and Italian migrants, for example, have been physically removed from French territory on these grounds.

Many individuals become forced migrants from outside the EU, such as refugees or internally displaced persons fleeing violence, due to environmental factors in relation to famine, chemical or nuclear disasters. Whatever their reasons for moving, forced migrants are frequently victims of border and asylum politics. Undocumented forced migrants are often positioned in other people's debates about securitisation and humanitarianism; discourses that generate policies create exclusion by categorising forced migrants as unwanted and undeserving strangers, with racial, national and religious stigmas imposed upon them. Their legal status is always questioned, as is their motivation to migrate, and deportation is a constant possibility. The public discussion of asylum is for the most part framed in terms of the advantages, disadvantages and potential threats that migrants may or may not bring to the host country.

The stranger is stigmatised because they represent an exception to the norm; their identity and common life experience constructed in relation to prejudicial attitudes, spatial and physical barriers, exclusionary institutions and limited access to resources. As the stranger may be unwilling or unable to fully engage with the definition of the situation they are much more likely to experience disqualification from full social acceptance and the imposition of a stigmatised identity. Drawing upon definition of the situation and frame, within any social setting categories of persons are established by the 'routines of social intercourse', the allocation of a person to a category provides the basis for our understanding of the person's social identity. The category also provides an understanding of the attributes that one should expect a person to have who has been allocated to each of these categories. The understanding of the attributes that a person should have allows all people who are co-present to anticipate how a person should behave. However, we do not always become aware of this process of categorisation or the assumptions we make about a person unless we come across a discrepancy that makes us question their actual social identity and how it may differ from our initial assumptions. In other words, if we suspect an individual is making false suppositions about themselves we may start to look for stigma symbols, namely signs which can be used to identify a discrepancy between an individual's actual social identity and their virtual identity. However, the act of concealing personal identity can have serious implications regarding the allocation of an individual to a social category (Goffman 1963a: 61).

Not all individuals who are seen to be normal are hostile towards the person with a stigma. Goffman identifies a category of persons whom he describes as the 'wise':

> persons who are normal but whose special situation has made them intimately privy to the secret life of the stigmatized individual and sympathetic with it .... Wise persons are the marginal men before whom the individual with a fault need, feel no shame nor exert self-control, knowing that in spite of his failing he will be seen as an ordinary other.
>
> *(Goffman 1963a: 28)*

The idea of personal identity for Goffman is based upon the idea that an individual is distinctive and as such can be set apart from all others. Personal identifiers are used to differentiate self from other, in that the self possesses: 'a single continuous record of social facts can be attached, entangled, like candy floss, becoming then the sticky substance to which still other biographical facts can be attached' (Goffman 1963a: 57).

Goffman's argument is that the stigmatised individual defines themselves as no different from any other human being, while the people with whom they are co-present define that person in negative terms as a person who is different. Within the definition of the situation there are 'advocated codes of conduct' that provide the stigmatised person with guidance as to how to deal with the others present. The code of conduct defines the stigmatised person as 'not really one of them' and provides them with guidelines for an appropriate attitude regarding their definition of self; what Goffman refers to as 'recipes of being' (Goffman 1963a: 111–112). Part of the code of conduct includes when it is appropriate to conform to 'disclosure etiquette' in relation to their stigma. Goffman gives the following example:

> A 37-year-old male whose face is grossly disfigured but who carries on a real estate business stated, 'When I have an appointment with a new contact, I try to manage to be standing at a distance and facing the door, so the person entering will have more time to see me and get adjusted to my appearance before we start talking'.
>
> *(Goffman 1963a: 118)*

It is not uncommon for social movements to emerge that have the political objective of attempting to redefine stigma as differentness (Goffman 1963a: 114), however it is made clear to the stigmatised individual that acceptance is conditional on their 'good adjustment' to the normalising constraints of the definition of the situation; in Goffman's words: 'A phantom acceptance is thus allowed to provide the base for a phantom normalcy' (Goffman 1963a: 122).

Conclusion

In this chapter it was argued that Goffman viewed social life as a form of interaction order that is constructed out of highly ritualised performances based upon dramaturgical practices. Goffman has identified two conceptions of the stranger: a person whom we gift with civil inattention as they appear to be skilled in 'doing normal', and a person whom we choose to categorise as strange in a negative and stigmatised sense claiming they are less competent at 'doing normal'. Both conceptions of the stranger in Goffman's work are products of the definition of the situation or frame. Engagement with the definition of the situation is central to social life but risky. Human agents are skilled in the 'defensive practices' used to protect their preferred identities and 'protective practices' that we can choose to deploy to support another person's definition of the situation. All people run the risk of becoming stigmatised as all people must present themselves in everyday life and that presentation can fail and all people can be seen to create a situational impropriety – the first stage in the moral career of becoming the stranger.

References

Bateson, G. (1972) A theory of play and phantasy. In *Steps to an ecology of mind* (pp. 177–193). Chicago: University of Chicago Press.

Berger, P. L. and T. Luckmann (1966) *The social construction of reality: A treatise in the sociology of knowledge*. Garden City, NY: Anchor Books.

Durkheim, E. (1953) *Sociology and philosophy*, trans. D. F. Pocock. London: Cohen and West.

Foucault, M. (1990/1984) *The use of pleasure, volume 2 of the History of sexuality*. New York: Vintage Books.

Garland-Thomson, R. (2011) Misfits: A feminist materialist disability concept. *Hypatia*, 26(3), 591–609.

Goffman, E. (1956) *Presentation of self in everyday life*. Edinburgh: University of Edinburgh Social Sciences Research Centre, The Bateman Press.

Goffman, E. (1956a) Embarrassment and social organization. *American Journal of Sociology*, 62(3), 264–271.

Goffman, E. (1959) *The presentation of self in everyday life*. Garden City, NY: Anchor Books.

Goffman, E. (1961) *Asylums: Essays on the social situation of mental patients and other inmates*. New York: Anchor Books Doubleday & Company.

Goffman, E. (1962) On cooling the mark out: Some aspects of adaptation to failure. In A. Rose (ed.), *Human behavior and social processes* (pp. 482–505). Boston, MA: Houghton Mifflin.

Goffman, E. (1963) *Behaviour in public places*. New York: The Free Press.

Goffman, E. (1963a) *Stigma: Notes on the management of a spoilt identity*. Englewood Cliffs, NJ: Prentice-Hall.

Goffman, E. (1964) The neglected situation, *American Anthropologist*, 66(62), 133–136.

Goffman, E. (1967) *Interaction ritual: On face to face behaviour*. New York: Pantheon Books. On face-work pp. 5–47.

Goffman, E. (1974) *Frame analysis*. Boston: North Western University Press.

James, W. (1950/1869) The perception of reality. In *Principles of psychology*, vol. 2 (pp. 283–324). New York: Dover Publications.

Lafleur, M. L. and Mescoli, E. (2018) Creating undocumented EU migrants through welfare: A conceptualization of undeserving and precarious citizenship. *Sociology*, 52(3), 480–496.

Mead, G. H. (1925) The genesis of the self and social control. *International Journal of Ethics*, 35(3), 251–277.

Mead, G. H. (1962/1934) *Mind, self, and society: From the standpoint of a social behaviourist*. Chicago: The University of Chicago Press.

Price, M. (2015) The bodymind problem and the possibilities of pain. *Hypatia*, 30(1), 270–284.

Sacks, H. (1984) On doing 'being ordinary'. In J. M. Atkinson and J. Heritage (eds), *Structures of social action: Studies in emotion and social interaction* (pp. 413–429). Cambridge: Cambridge University Press.

Scheibe, K. E. (2002) *The drama of everyday life*. Cambridge MA: Harvard University Press.

Schutz, A. (1962/1945) On multiple realities. In *Collected papers*, 3 vols (1, 207–259.) The Hague: Martinus Nijhoff.

Thomas, W. I. (1923) *The unadjusted girl. With cases and standpoint for behavior analysis*. Boston, MA: Little, Brown.

United Nations High Commissioner for Refugees (UNHCR) (2015). Worldwide displacement hits all-time high as war and persecution increase. http://www.unhcr.org/news/latest/2015/6/558193896/worldwide-displacement-hits-all-time-high-war-persecution-increase.html

United Nations High Commissioner for Refugees (UNHCR) (2017). Syria regional refugee response. Retrieved 23 February 2017, from: http://data.unhcr.org/syrianrefugees/regional.php

5

THE *BANLIEUE*

Pierre Bourdieu and the excluded urban poor

From a Bourdieusian perspective, estrangement comes into being in the first instance because of the unequal allocation of capital resources within society. Either the stranger has insufficient capital to enter the social field or their relative lack of capital means that they are unable to secure a position within the field and as such their position is not regarded as legitimate. Although he did not often directly address the issue of the stranger, in his *Sketch for a Self-Analysis* Bourdieu (2008) attempts to interrogate his own feelings of transgression and his own feelings of hysteresis. He attempts to identify what generated the conflictive relations he experienced and why he felt estranged and defined as 'not belonging'; caught between an 'institutional habitus' and a 'family habitus'. What if anything underpinned Bourdieu's sense of transgression; why did he feel as if he were stepping outside the boundary lines of containment within the given habitus, not following accepted norms or accepted practice? By exceeding boundaries Bourdieu stood between habitus or within the habitus clivé and found himself, like other strangers, in an unfamiliar or uncomfortable space and faced with potentially uncomfortable consequences.

This chapter will explore the link that Bourdieu explores between practice and the precarious life that excluded people, such as those who became seen as a *racaille* experience. There is a body of philosophical work developed initially by Bourdieu and later by theorists, notably Julia Kristeva, Giorgio Agamben and Judith Butler, which indicates that life under neo-liberalism has become increasingly precarious, characterised by a greater sense of abjection, and feelings of permanent liminality and uncertainty. The term 'precariat' was first used by Bourdieu to characterise the unforeseen human consequence of neoliberal economic reforms. It describes a situation of estrangement generated by material and psychological vulnerability, exploitation and lack of security brought about by the changing nature of social inequalities. From Bourdieu (1997, 1999) onwards, precarity has been used to suggest a generalised state of material and emotional insecurity that cuts across traditional socio-economic divisions.

In contrast to the criticism of Bourdieu's earlier work from Jeffrey Alexander, amongst others, that Bourdieu demotes culture to a reflection of particular social structures and undervalued individual human agency in favour of structure and symbolic aspects of confrontation with the powerful in the field, Alexander (1995: 137) argues that symbolic codes for Bourdieu are nothing more than the: 'immediate reflections of the hierarchical structures of material life'. The criticism here is that because of Bourdieu's emphasis on the unconscious incorporation of objective structures, this leaves little room for human agency to break the pattern of domination within the Habitus. In an interview with Terry Eagleton in 1991, Bourdieu explains that in the Marxian analysis: 'the capacity for resistance, as a capacity of consciousness, was overestimated' (Bourdieu and Eagleton 1995: 268). Bourdieu also explains how in his own work he substitutes the concepts of symbolic violence and symbolic domination for the word ideology to explain that like other people he has 'difficulty formulating my thoughts. I am under a strong form of symbolic violence which is related to the face that language is not mine' (Bourdieu and Eagleton 1995: 266). Symbolic violence is defined by Wacquant (1998a: 217) as: 'the imposition of systems of meaning that legitimize and thus solidity structures of inequality'. For Bourdieu, how the social world works is based on practice not consciousness. In addition, the concept of doxa is used to explain how people 'accept things without knowing them' (Bourdieu and Eagleton 1995: 268) and Bourdieu explains that doxa operates below the level of consciousness. In other words that culture is simply a reflection of the class structure for Bourdieu. In contrast, in *Sketch for a Self-Analysis*, Bourdieu (2008) is concerned with the individual voice. He moves away from his earlier position that is assumed to undervalue individual human agency by attempting to understand himself by drawing upon his own contribution to social analysis as a form of self-analysis.

Strangers are often new entrants into the field. Their lack of knowledge, capital and understanding of practice make them marginalised people from a Bourdieu perspective, and this marginalisation is rooted in a form of symbolic violence exercised by the more skilled and established inhabitants of the field who see the new entrants as not belonging and who fear that the new entrants will redefine the culture to suit their own ends. In these circumstances the excluded and marginalised individual must find another field in which they feel both comfortable and welcome as an authentic participant. Bourdieu applies his sociology to examine the social divisions and urban problems in contemporary France.

The Weight of the World

Drawing upon extensive recordings and transcriptions of the voices of the urban poor, *The Weight of the World* (Bourdieu 1999) is concerned with attempting to understand the experiences of the vulnerable living in the urban environment, and their social exclusion brought about by poor housing, underemployment, unemployment and inter-racial conflict. *The Weight of the World* is Bourdieu's critique of the French government's policy in relation to the urban poor; a policy that he describes as active exclusion of people who become identified as undesirable. Bourdieu argues that when 'right-minded people' are asked about the urban environment and the people who live there, they respond emotionally by drawing upon tabloid representations of the inhabitants and political propaganda. Many of us have internalised the negative media representations of the urban poor. For the inhabitants of poor neighbourhoods, the social space of the urban environment can be experienced as having impassable, solid social boundaries that restrict access to social and symbolic resources. As Patrick

Champagne (56) explains in one of his contributions to *The Weight of the World*, the role of the media is to define how to place individuals within any social problem:

> [T]he media now form an integral part of reality, or if you prefer, produce reality effects by creating a media-oriented vision of reality that contributes to creating the reality it claims to describe. In particular, misfortunes and social demands now have to be expressed through the media to have any hope of having a publicly recognized existence and to be, in one way or another, 'taken into account' by those with political power.
>
> *(Bourdieu 1999: 56)*

Social agents are constituted in, and in relationship to, a social space. As such they are situated in a social space and that social space is translated into physical space with positive or negative (stigmatising) properties with what people consider within the field to be a 'natural frontier'. Neil Fligstein and Doug McAdam explain that fields: 'are focused on the emergence, stabilization/institutionalization, and transformation of socially constructed arenas in which embedded actors compete for material and status rewards' (Fligstein and McAdam 2012: 5).

Membership of the field is based upon subjective 'standing' within the field rather than any objective criteria. The boundaries of strategic action within the field are not fixed. Finally, fields are constructed out of a set of understandings formed over time by members of the field themselves. Stability within the field is commonly accomplished by the imposition of hierarchical power. The field can develop, and 'institutional logic' by which consensus within the field about what is going on helps to shape the position of individuals by the creation of rules that favour the more powerful over the less powerful. The purpose and structure of the field can become shaped to the interests of the powerful (Fligstein and McAdam 2012: 10–13).

With strategic action understood by Fligstein and McAdam (2012: 17) as the attempt by individuals, through the creation of identities, social skills and framing the course of action, 'to create and sustain social worlds by securing the cooperation of others', the field is then a structured space of positions, which reifies and inscribes spatial distance into a social distance. Stigmatised properties become objectified within physical space. The possession of capital makes it possible to keep undesirable persons and things at a distance:

> Conversely, those who are deprived of capital are either physically or symbolically held at a distance from goods that are the rarest socially; they are forced to stick with the most undesirable and the least rare persons or goods. The lack of capital intensifies the experience of finitude: it chains one to a place.
>
> *(Bourdieu 1999: 127)*

The political construction of space favours the construction of homo-geneous groups on a spatial basis and this is largely responsible for the creation of state-funded housing projects that become run-down areas of cities. Such spaces become stigmatised areas that symbolically degrade the inhabitants. Bourdieu came to this view after conducting extensive interviews to listen to the voices of the urban poor in the cities or *banlieue*; people who are rarely listened to, to understand their structural position, or habitus. These ideas have been taken up in the United States and France by Loïc Wacquant with his concept of *The Zone*.

The key conceptual shifts in Bourdieu's understanding of the class structure, identified by Wacquant (2013), include the transition from class consciousness to habitus, ideology to symbolic violence, and from ruling class to field of power. This shift suggests that in his later work Bourdieu lost faith in analytical usefulness of class as a conceptual tool. However, he remained focused on developing his understanding of inequality. By 2000 Bourdieu wanted to 'shun the use of the word "ideology"' because the concept largely ignored the 'naturalisation' of categories of belief that comes about because of the 'inscription of the social in things and in bodies', including inscription of belief in the bodies of the dominant and of the dominated. This form of inscription was for Bourdieu one of 'the most powerful mechanisms of the main-tenance of the symbolic order' (Bourdieu 2000: 177). Bourdieu's understanding of social exclusion became more clearly rooted in a sense of habitus clivé, the symbolic fabrication of collectivities and the struc-tured and structuring position of the excluded within any field or social space. Bourdieu's approach to understanding exclusion within a field became more akin to Goffman's conception of 'sense of placement' and drew explicitly on the Eliasian conception of incorporation.

Practice

Bourdieu's theory of practice is an attempt to reconcile the dualism(s) found within philosophy and social science between agency and structure, structuralism and constructivism and free will and determinism: 'objectivism universalizes the theorist's relation to the objective of science, so subjectivism universalizes the experience that the subject of theoretical discourse has of theoretical discourse has of himself as a subject' (Bourdieu 1990: 45–46). In contrast to phenomenology, the 'natural attitude' within the world of lived experience is a socially constructed perceptual scheme made possible by the acquisition of the habitus and of dispositions demanded by a field that are part of a complex process of socialisation and not a mechanical or simple process such as the imposition of 'character' onto an individual by the use constraint.

Bourdieu developed John Dewey's pragmatism, for sociological purposes. Dewey rejected the dualistic epistemology and metaphysics of modern philosophy. Like Dewey, Bourdieu argued that our experience does not reflect upon itself; experience is regarded as taken for granted and self-evident; to understand practice means that we must step outside of our practice and question those ways of behaving that have become internalised. Bourdieu's theory of practice underpins his analysis of social reality. The main elements of Bourdieu's theory of practice initially emerged from his research into the Kabyle peoples in Algeria in the late 1950s and early 1960s. For Bourdieu practice is a form of human activity found in the field, with the field seen as a spatial metaphor that describes a conceptual space of shared meaning or generative scheme between subjectivity and objectivity. Practice is focused on the ways in which human agents choose to repeat aspects of social life to the degree that such patterns become internalised (which Bourdieu terms *illusio*) and develop into actions that are durable enough to become difficult for any single individual to change. The practices of agents are not arbitrary, and practice gives social life an expected or rule-like quality. Practice links the inner world of subjectivity to the outer world of regulation or habitus. Moreover, it is practice that connects individual thought and individual social action in the process of transition from individual habit to habitus. Practice can be viewed as providing the individual with a 'stylistic unity' or a 'taste' that makes their choices have a predictable quality.

Interaction between people takes place within the field; and within the field individual people must draw upon the capital resources available to them to find a position in which they feel both competent and secure. Bourdieu uses the term doxa to identify the individual's taken for granted knowledge of the field upon which practice is based within the field. The field is then a site of struggle and it is the overcoming of this struggle that is central leading to reproduction of practice within the field.

Bourdieu's theory of practice is built on the relationship between three concepts: habitus, field and capital. The interaction between these concepts guides human agency in terms of thinking, feeling and perceiving and directs practice. Habitus are:

> systems of durable, transposable dispositions, structured structures predisposed to function as structuring structures, that is, as principles which generate and organize practices and representations that can be objectively adapted to their outcomes without presupposing a conscious aiming at ends or an express mastery of the operations necessary in order to attain them. Objectively 'regulated' and 'regular' without being in any way the product of obedience to rules, they can be collectively orchestrated without being the product of the organizing action of a conductor.
>
> *(Bourdieu 1990: 53)*

In summary, Bourdieu uses the concept of the habitus to construct a theory of practice that draws upon the concepts of agency and habit, derived from John Dewey's pragmatism. Habitus allows the individual to have an active engagement with the past that informs the individual on the appropriate way to behave within the present. Habitus helps to shape our perception, our thoughts, and action. Divergent groups have divergent practices derived from divergent habitus. Habitus operates in combination with capital and field. Capital can take a variety of forms: economic, social, cultural, symbolic. The field is viewed by Bourdieu as an environment that can be physical, institutional or perceptual in which competitive exchanges for resources take place. The field for Bourdieu is the field of struggle in which people compete for capital within an oppressive and exploitative situation:

> A field is a structured social space, a field of forces, a force field. It contains people who dominate and others who are dominated. Constant, permanent relationships of inequality operate inside this space, which at the same time becomes a space in which the various actors struggle for the transformation or preservation of the field. All the individuals in this universe bring to the competition all the (relative) power at their disposal. It is this power that defines their position in the field and, as a result, their strategies.
>
> *(Bourdieu 2011: 40-41)*

Habitus

Habitus emerges from the class relations and structures of power that produce it. The habitus generates common sense and is viewed by Bourdieu as a system that allows individuals to believe that the social world already exists. Habitus contains cognitive structures that the individual can draw upon to support their motivation. Past experiences can be made sense of by placing an experience into the appropriate cognitive structure 'deposited in each organism in the form of schemes of perception, thought and action' (Bourdieu 1990: 54).

The connection between Bourdieu's understanding of the connection between 'structuring structures' (habitus) and individual subjective experience and interpretation of the world is underpinned by his conception of practice. Our making sense of self is the product of a social process. Different social classes generate different habitus that allow practices to become harmonised between people who share the same class position. Within the habitus class-based practices are formed. People who share the same class position share similar experiences and the individuals may not be aware of the influence of the habitus on their everyday thoughts and actions, as the habitus is deeply unconscious for Bourdieu but it: 'enables practices to be objectively harmonized without any calculation or conscious reference … or explicit co-ordination' (Bourdieu 1990: 58–59).

Capital

Bourdieu identifies four types of capital: economic capital, cultural capital, social capital and symbolic capital (Bourdieu 1986) and different fields value different forms of capital. However, the possession of economic capital is central to Bourdieu's understanding of power in capitalist society. By the same token, the possession of any form of capital allows the owner to exercise some power and advantage over people who possess relatively less capital. Social capital is concerned with the relationships that an individual has with others who possess capital and the ability of the individual to make use of these relationships to secure a comparative advantage. Cultural capital is an embodied form of capital reflected in the possession of good taste, the understanding of culture and the ability to articulate concepts and ideas. Cultural capital is reflected in qualifications that are valued in the wider society in the form of status and prestige.

Symbolic violence

Symbolic violence is incorporated within the processes of class formation, it is a subtle form of discrimination that is used to prevent individuals from entering a given field or attempting to challenge the dominant position of people within the habitus. Symbolic violence is used to bring about social closure: the exclusion of individuals from the field as a mechanism to reduce competition for capital resources within the habitus. For most of the time, inequalities in capitalist societies are maintained by forms of symbolic domination rather than by resort to physical force: 'exerted for the most part … through the purely symbolic channels of communication and cognition … recognition or even feeling' (Bourdieu 2001: 2). Symbolic violence is a 'gentle invisible form of violence' (Bourdieu 1977:192) and the symbolic channels of communication and cognition are the mundane processes or practices of everyday life. It is form of violence: 'which is exercised upon a social agent with his or her complicity' (Bourdieu and Wacquant 1992: 167).

For Bourdieu one of the weaknesses of the traditional Marxian approach to power is the absence of a concept of the symbolic: '[symbolic] violence can do what political and police violence can do, but more efficiently' (Bourdieu and Wacquant 1992: 166).

As Bourdieu made clear, the excluded were complicit in their domination:

> Any symbolic domination presupposes on the part of those who are subjected to it a form of complicity which is neither a passive submission to an external constraint nor a free adherence to values …. The specificity of symbolic violence resides precisely in the fact that it requires of the person who undergoes it an attitude which defies the ordinary alternative between freedom and constraint.
>
> *(Bourdieu 1982: 36 cited in Bourdieu and Wacquant 1992: 168)*

From Bourdieu's perspective all domination has a symbolic element to it, even when domination is imposed by force or money there is always a symbolic dimension, reflected in an act of submission, obedience or recognition. In a fashion reminiscent of Butler's account of the link between the lord and the bondsman, for Bourdieu symbolic capital:

> enables forms of domination which imply dependence on those who can be dominated by it, since it only exists through the esteem, recognition, belief, credit, confidence of others, and can only be perpetuated so long as it succeeds in obtaining belief in its existence.
>
> *(Bourdieu 2000: 166)*

At a practical level the people who impose symbolic violence expect the dominated to silently contribute to their own domination by implicitly accepting, in advance, the limits imposed on them, by exhibiting shame, anxiety and guilt made possible by the habituation. The processes of exclusion as estrangement are not exerted by a knowing consciousness but are built into the schemes of perception provided within the habitus. Domination using symbolic violence is the product of the incorporation of what have become understood as the natural or naturalized classifications by which an individual makes sense of their social being. The incorporation of symbolic violence into self allows a person to say this is me and I am one of you. Symbolic violence is then the coercion through the consent of the dominated: 'exerted not in the pure logic of knowing consciousnesses but in the obscurity of the dispositions of habitus, in which are embedded the schemes of perception and appreciation which, below the level of the decisions of the conscious mind' (Bourdieu 2000: 170–171).

Incorporation

The process of incorporation becomes engrained into all the state's citizens or subjects. Incorporation is the foundation of 'common sense' and consensus. Incorporation defines the relationships and the boundaries between agents within the habitus. The processes of incorporation underpin the practical knowledge and understanding, in the form of emotion that defines a person's 'sense of one's place' within the habitus. The emotion also underpins the sense of unease we feel when someone appears to be out of place with the habitus. Incorporation is then understood by Bourdieu as structuring imposed on practices by the State that:

> institutes and inculcates common symbolic forms of thought, social frames of perception, understanding or memory, State forms of classification, becomes immanent to all its 'subjects' .... The symbolic order is based on the imposition on all agents of structuring structures which derive part of their consistency and resistance to the fact that they are, in appearance at least, coherent and systematic.
>
> *(Bourdieu 2000: 175–176)*

A key element of this process is the 'pre-reflexive' and unconscious 'doxic submission' of the individual human agent, that is the submission of the individual's intellectual processes, including belief and opinion: 'which binds us to the established order .... The doxic submission of the dominated to the objective structures of a social order of which their cognitive structures are the product' (Bourdieu 2000: 177).

Pre-reflexive is understood by Bourdieu as thought embedded without awareness within practical activity. The state does not necessarily need to make use of coercion to produce an ordered social world, because the state can: 'produce incorporated cognitive structures attuned to the objective structures and so secure doxic submission to the established order' (Bourdieu 2000: 178).

The habitus reproduces itself using the conscious or unconscious actions of people whose role is that of active producers who are described as 'true agents'. The exercise of human agency is the product of the structure that they, the human agents themselves, help to reproduce in the future. Reproduction of the habitus is described by Bourdieu as taking place because 'agents': 'internalized the immanent law of the structure' (Bourdieu and Wacquant 1992: 140). However, Bourdieu came to dislike the phrase 'immanent law of the structure' and preferred to describe internalisation as 'a universal and universally realized norm of adequate practice' (Bourdieu and Wacquant 1992: 124).

Habitus clivé

Within the field individuals draw upon capital to construct boundaries between individual and social groups to whom they belong and arrange them hierarchically. However, when an individual moves between fields, the habitus they were initially socialised into may no longer be advantageous. Estrangement can in Bourdieu be experienced as a divided habitus (habitus clivé).

Estrangement can be a product of the experience of hysteresis. In 'Reproduction' Bourdieu and Passeron (1977: 175) explain that: 'practices can be adjusted to their position in the system without being directly governed by anything other than the reinterpretation, offered by the system, of the objective conditions of their presence in the system'. From this position practice is shaped by habitus and changes in practice are guided by the habitus itself. When a person is mobile either social or geographically there is the very real possibility that the individual will experience a mismatch between their original habitus and the new habitus that they find themselves in. In his later work Bourdieu focused more closely on the individual effects of changes in habitus and practice and explains that human agents apply categories of perception based upon their previous experience to make sense of the world. However, even minor changes within the habitus can generate misrecognition or false beliefs (allodoxia), as Bourdieu explains: 'When structures are modified, even slightly, the structural hysteresis of the categories of perception and appreciation gives rise to diverse forms of allodoxia' (Bourdieu 1998: 219). The experience of hysteresis can then be one of isolation and estrangement.

In terms of understanding the possible link between estrangement and hysteresis, Bourdieu's concept of a divided habitus, or habitus clivé, is useful for understanding the process of estrangement, by which people break the conventions of doxa leading to misrecognition of their behaviour and even a fragmentation of self. Moreover, as suggested above, Bourdieu used the conception of habitus clivé in his own self-analysis to make sense of his feeling of disconnection between his home background and his experience of social mobility and the academic circles that he inhabited in later life:

> [A]s a result of the hysteresis effect necessarily implied in the logic of the constitution of habitus, practices are always liable to incur negative sanctions when the environment with which they are actually confronted is too distant from that to which they are objectively fitted.
>
> *(Bourdieu 1978: 78)*

For Bourdieu, knowledge and perception are social constructions. Practices are cognitive and motivational structures that make up the habitus. The hysteresis effect is understood as a change or adjustment between the habitus and the social context, to the degree that people must rethink their position within the habitus. The situation has much in common with the situation within families when children have aspirations that are not matched by those of their parents:

> The product of such a contradictory injunction is doomed .... Such experiences tend to produce a habitus divided against itself, in constant negotiation with itself and with its ambivalence, and

therefore doomed to a kind of duplication, to a double perception of self, to successive allegiances and multiple identities.

(Bourdieu 1999: 510–511)

Loïc Wacquant: from social state to penal state

Since the 1980s small scale riots have occurred in French cités (low-income, subsidised housing) and *banlieue* (housing projects that were built from the 1960s onwards to provide housing for working-class white people and the pied-noirs, the French citizens who left North Africa after the Algerian War of Independence). Fabien Jobard (2014) has listed violent outbreaks occurring in Mantes-la-Jolie (1991), Sartrouville (1992), Melun (1993), Paris (1993, 2005, 2007 and also in 2018 and 2019), Dammarie-lès-Lys (1997), Toulouse (1998), Lille (2001), Montfermeil (2006), Villiers le-Bel (2007), Saint Dizier (2007), Grigny (2008), Romans-sur-Isère (2008), Woippy (2010), Clermont-Ferrand and Amiens (2012) and Trappes (2013). These disturbances usually involve the destruction of public buildings, violent confrontation with riot police and the burning of cars. Jobard (2014) and other commentators have described such violence as a mode of protest initiated by deprived youths on deprived estates who regard themselves as people without a conventional political voice and who consequently reject both compromise and conventional politics to gain some political or economic advantage.

The 2005 disturbances began on 27 October 2005, in Clichy-sous-Bois, a suburb of Seine-St-Denis in the north-east of Paris, after three youths, Bouna Traoré (aged 15), Zyed Benna (aged 17) and Muttin Altun (aged 17), ran away from the police and, in an effort to escape, jumped over the fence of an electric transformer. Bouna and Zyed were electrocuted and died at the scene; Muttin was seriously burned but managed to make his escape. Overnight there were disturbances in Clichy-sous-Bois with several cars burned, a nursery school, some local shops and bus shelters set on fire. The events sparked civil unrest in suburban housing projects across France.

After the rioting by youths in October and November 2005, the then Interior Minister Nicolas Sarkozy described the people involved in the disturbances as *racaille* and threatened to 'pressure wash' the cites ('cleaned up with a Kärcher'). According to the *Le Petit Robert* (Robert Dictionary of the French Language), *racaille* is a derogatory term meaning 'contemptible populace', 'rejects of society', despicable or vulgar people. Most importantly from a Bourdieu perspective the term *la racaille* is more readily used to categorise types of people in an accusatory and moralising manner, rather than to describe the behaviours of specific individuals.

Following the 2007 riots, in a speech to 2,000 gendarmes and policemen in Paris, the then President Nicolas Sarkozy dismissed the actions of the people involved in the incidents: 'What happened in Villiers-le-Bel has nothing to do with a social crisis. It has everything to do with a "thugocracy".' He continued by saying: 'I reject any form of other-worldly naivety that wants to see a victim of society in anyone who breaks the law, a social problem in any riot.' He maintained: 'The response to the riots isn't yet more money on the backs of the tax-payers. The response to the riots is to arrest the rioters .... We'll give more to those who want to get ahead honestly' (cited in Samuel 2007).

Sarkozy attempted to promote the moral position within dominant French discourse that the *racaille* are contaminated and contaminating and their presence in France and their maintenance of North African and Muslim beliefs threatens the purity of public space. Eric Macé (2005) observes that Sarkozy attempted to blame the people in the cités and *banlieue* for their own plight without relating the events to his own neo-liberal policies and their impact on the wider socio-economic conditions in the urban environment. For Macé, Sarkozy's stance was like: 'accusing the rioters of the Commune of Paris in 1870 who revolted against the bourgeoisie which had made alliance with the German troops occupying France'. There is also little doubt that Sarkozy had immigrants in general, and Muslims in particular, in mind when making his comments. He was reported by the BBC as having said that there are too many foreigners in France and the system for integrating them is 'working worse and worse' (BBC 2012).

Sarkozy also had a public disagreement with respected film maker Mathieu Kassovitz over his comments. Life in the *banlieue* had been depicted in Mathieu Kassovitz's critically acclaimed (1995) film *La Haine*; a film that gave an informed reflection of the racial and social issues that people faced in the *banlieue*. However, despite the critical response to Sarkozy's comments, according to Chantal Tetreault (2008: 144): 'As in dominant French discourse, the figure of la *racaille* has come to be emblematic for the stigmatized urban spaces of cités among their inhabitants.'

Precarity

In the Thatcher/Regan era there was a clear attempt to promote individualism and a reclassification of inequality away from social class. Poverty and inequality were seen to persist, but people were encouraged to view themselves as having an individual identity rather than a class-based identity and the causes of inequality were increasingly seen to be a product of personal failing rather than a product of class inequality. By the late 1990s the perception of the poor as the strangers within, a pathological, abject, irresponsible, dirty underclass, was established within popular culture. Clear division was established: 'between the "deserving poor" and the rest, who [are] morally condemned for their fecklessness and immorality' (Bourdieu 2000: 79).

The terms 'precariat', 'precarious' and 'precarity' describe a situation of material and psychological vulnerability, uncertainty and lack of security brought about by the changing nature of social inequalities in neo-liberalism. The term precarity was first use by Bourdieu (1977) to suggest a generalised state of material and emotional insecurity that cuts across traditional socio-economic divisions. Taking his point of departure from Bourdieu (1997), Loïc Wacquant has investigated the urban poor who have become a section of the population beneath the proletariat; a form of contemporary lumpen proletariat who face difficulties finding secure employment. Precarity is experienced not only as economic exclusion but as a highly personal condition that brings about a disaffection with self. As Judith Butler (2004: 15) explains, it is a condition in which individuals question their self-sovereignty: 'I am other to myself precisely at the place where I expect to be myself.'

The state of material and emotional insecurity generated by precarity is experienced in a similar fashion to Gregor Samsa, the central character on Franz Kafka's novella *The Metamorphosis*: 'One morning, upon awakening from agitated dreams, Gregor Samsa found himself, in his bed, transformed into a monstrous vermin' (Kafka 1915: 1). Gregor wakes up to discover he has turned into a giant insect, however none of the characters seeks an explanation as to what brought about Gregor's transformation. As such the transformation appears to be without cause or reason. Moreover, Gregor himself never attempts to find out how or why he was transformed. Kafka presents Gregor as the victim of an evidently purposeless and random metamorphosis, which is the product of context in which things irrational and chaotic happen without our full understanding. In the first part of the story when Gregor is still attempting to turn over and open the door, the transformation totally changes his appearance, and although Gregor is unable to communicate his thoughts and feelings to his family, his sense of whom he is remains unchanged. Once the door is opened his family develops a psychological distance towards him and even his sister's initial feelings of sympathy towards him turn to revulsion. Gregor becomes excluded and eventually accepts his separation from humanity.

In his work on the urban poor, Wacquant builds upon the 'cultural turn' in class analysis initiated by Bourdieu to argue that precariousness is directly linked to neo-liberal policies of austerity and patterns of global capital accumulation. Wacquant suggests that what is 'neo' about neoliberalism is a successful strategy of 'reengineering and redeployment of the state as the core agency that sets the rules and fabricates the subjectivities, social relations and collective representations suited to realising markets' (Wacquant 2012: 66).

Precaritisation transforms the collective identity of the poorest into a sub-proletariat; a group who are categorised as permanent outsiders or strangers to affluent society. The urban poor have become socially and geographically isolated, leading a precarious life characterised by unemployment and underemployment. However, precarity is not randomly distributed in contemporary society. Moreover, precariousness is not simply an economic condition. To lead a precarious life is to lead a life in a situation where one feels an overwhelming sense of vulnerability and dislocation, reflected in feelings of loneliness, isolation and uncertainty.

Drawing on Erving Goffman's (1963) analysis of stigma and Pierre Bourdieu's (1991) theory of group-formation, Loïc Wacquant (2007) stresses the significance of territorial stigmatisation and policy responses to issues of the material problems facing the new urban poor. For

Wacquant (2007), black neighbourhoods in the United States and the *banlieue* in French cities are increasingly occupied by a fragment of sub-proletariats who experience distinctive spatial levels of 'advanced marginality' – territorial fixation and stigmatisation, spatial alienation and the dissolution of 'place', and the loss of a hinterland. Since the 1990s Wacquant has argued that the urban environment is no longer 'civilized' in the way that Nobert Elias had suggested. The intersection of poverty, persistent joblessness, social deprivation and ethno-racial conflict has generated a new and distinct form of estrangement. Within the *banlieue*, a group have emerged who are increasingly isolated from the wider society and have become the new face of marginality in the urban environment. In both the United States and Europe the urban environment has become increasing polarised with the urban poor becoming increasingly stigmatised, supernumerary and subjected to a process of ghettoization in which they are forced into urban enclaves, in close proximity to the affluent cosmopolitan bourgeoisie but leading distinct and separate lives. Low paid, low skilled employment opportunities have declined for young people within the urban environment generating a process of deproletarianization:

> Rather than being diffused throughout working class areas, advanced marginality tends to concentrate in well-identified, bounded, and increasingly isolated territories viewed by both outsiders and insiders as social purgatories, urban hellholes where only the refuse of society would accept to dwell. A stigma of place thus superimposes itself on the already pervasive stigmata of poverty and (where applicable) of race or colonial-immigrant origin, as these 'penalized spaces' are, or threaten to become, permanent.
>
> *(Wacquant 1996: 125)*

The 'penalized spaces' were later described by Wacquant as the dark ghetto: 'the stigmatized territory where the fearsome "underclass," mired in immorality and welfare dependency, was said to have coalesced under the press of deindustrialization and social isolation to become one of the country's most urgent topics of public worry' (Wacquant 2009: 62).

People within the *banlieue* inhabit a zone of permanent social liminality; a life of symbolic and social fragmentation. As we saw in Chapter 3 on Bauman's conception of the stranger, the concept of liminality was initially devised by Arnold van Gennep (1960/1908) and later elaborated by Victor Turner (1967, 1969). Liminality emerges during historical phases of social and cultural transition when the stability of social life is questioned. Liminality reflects a precarious period in which individuals are perceived to be on the margins of society. Liminality is not solely an economic experience but an experience that heightens personal anxiety, impacts on the subjectivity of the individual and places the individual outside of human interrelatedness. For Wacquant the *banlieue* are marginalised in that they lose both their sense of connection with the traditional working class and their sense of locale; forced by economic necessity into decaying neighbourhoods and having to live alongside residents they do not want to be associated with. Many residents avoid contact with their neighbours to the degree that they lose a sense of place that they can identify with or feel secure within.

In terms of the social policy response to this form of marginalisation, the hyperghetto serves as a dumping ground for supernumerary categories of people for which the affluent society no longer has any economic or political use. Wacquant argues that there has been a shift from the social welfare initiatives to challenge social exclusion and marginalisation to a policy of criminalisation of poverty; with evermore punitive forms of management. A penal regulation of social insecurity that is focused on strengthening of the police and criminal justice system, and increasing the prison population, incarceration is used to physically neutralise the poor, take them off the street and 'warehouse' them to prevent offending. A central aspect is the penalisation of poverty, by which the marginalised themselves are blamed for their marginal position.

Wacquant presents his argument in *Punishing the Poor* as filling in a gap in Bourdieu's model presented in *The Weight of the World* by inserting a central role to the police, the criminal justice system and the prison as: 'core constituents of the "Right hand" of the state, alongside the ministries of the economy and the budget' (Wacquant 2009: 289). The role of this 'right hand' is one of coping with the entrenched poverty by the use of punitive containment.

Wacquant's (1996) solution to the *banlieue's* marginal position is to have a policy of decriminalisation and decarceration, and to decouple income security from employment by introducing a guaranteed minimum income, enough to provide subsistence and facilitate social participation. This basic income should be given to all individual members of society unconditionally without a means test or a requirement to work.

Wacquant (2001, 1996) argues that Norbert Elias's figurational approach is potentially useful in constructing an explanation for the transition from communal ghetto of the mid-twentieth century to the contemporary conception of the hyperghetto generated by the neo-liberal policies of social abandonment and punitive containment that have led to the collapse of public institutions and replacement of social safety nets by police and prisons; a policy that, according to Wacquant, has a tendency to reinforce the socioeconomic instability and inter-personal violence. Elias' framework can help: 'overcome some of the perennial limitations of conventional analyses of the conundrum of race and class in the U.S. metropolis' (Wacquant 2004: 111).

Contemporary society is experiencing a reversal of the civilizing process; a de-civilizing of the segregated core of large US cities reflected in a de-pacification of society, an environment of pandemic violence and the decline of businesses, churches, neighbourhood associations and public services. These developments have led to a shortening of net-works of interdependency. Wacquant's (1998) article 'Inside the Zone' opens with a description of a car journey in central Chicago and Wacquant's depiction of the poverty and dilapidated state of the buildings in the Wentworth district of the city. The argument that Wacquant presents is based upon an interview with boxer Rickey in a gym in downtown Chicago. Rickey is described as a 'professional hus-tler'. Rickey's account is supplemented with empirical data from reli-able sources such as *The Chicago Community Fact Book* (Kitagawa and Taeuber 1985) and other research. Wacquant explains that to hustle is to draw upon a form of symbolic capital based upon the ability to manipulate others for financial gain within the ghetto or as Rickey describes it 'Inside the Zone'. Without a 'legit' job, the activities that the hustler engages are never fully or completely legal and income streams are irregular. Part of the skill of the successful hustler is to sus-tain an 'elusive and slippery character' (Wacquant 1998: 3), a person who maintains a balance of seduction and coercion whilst 'playing it cool'.

The ghetto is described by Wacquant as quasi-carceral in nature; the ghetto is not suffering from social disorganisation but 'constitutes a dependent universe' that is 'differentiated and hierarchized' and based upon regulative principles, an: 'environment of pandemic violence and relentless material precariousness' (Wacquant 1998: 13). Wacquant explains that for the inhabitants of the ghetto marginalisation has become part of the order of things.

The penal state approach views the *banlieue*'s marginal position as due to their deviant values and behavioural patterns. The *banlieue* are assumed to lack the psychological and psycho-social attributes that are understood to be necessary to participate in polite society. Consequently, the *banlieue* are always 'out-of-place', abject, assumed to be undeserving and excluded. Unlike traditional forms of poverty that are often residual, cyclical or transitional, the marginal position of the *banlieue* signals the formation of the 'precariat'; a group of individuals who live in an abject state of permanent liminality, regarded as the dangerous strangers within, a socially alien and hostile underclass, an 'undeserving poor' characterised by their 'anti-social' impulses and pathological life style. The inner city has become a 'penalised space' in which residents' lives are characterised by and experienced through a dire sense of indignity. Wacquant (2007) is surprised that Erving Goffman (1963a) did not identify place of residence as one of the forms of stigma that can exclude the individual from aspects of social life and deprive them from full acceptance by others. To live in a penalised space has much in common with the three types of stigma detailed by Goffman; as to be stigmatised by place contaminates all members of a family:

Les Minguettes and La Courneuve or the Mirail housing complex in Toulouse for France; South Central Los Angeles, the Bronx and the project of Cabrini Green in Chicago for the United States; Duisberg-Marxloh and Berlin-Neukölln for Germany; the districts of Toxteth in Liverpool, Saint Paul in Bristol, or Meadow Well in Newcastle for England; and Bijlmer and Westlijke Tuinsteden in Amsterdam for Holland.

(Wacquant 2007: 68)

These areas and other are identified by Wacquant (2007: 68, 72) as: 'zones reserved for the urban outcasts', 'human rejects' or the precariat; people who live on insecure fringes of the proletariat, negatively defined by social privation and 'compelled to form its subjectivity out of its objectification' by others.

'Chavs' and ideologies of decline

As we have seen, for Bourdieu class struggle is more than a simple matter of access to both economic and cultural resources. In the state-sponsored process of neoliberal class decomposition, the recreation and redefinition of poverty as a personal failing has become reflected regularly in popular culture by stigmatising depictions of people living in poverty. In the English context, the term 'chav' has been used to mock and deride poorer people with white working-class origins as the non-respectable working class, talentless, immoral and undeserving. People who are seen to be vulgar, violent and lacking in taste (Tyler and Bennett 2010). 'Chavs' are the abject and underserving working-class people who are said to lead a 'shameless' lifestyle. *Shameless* was a critically acclaimed and popular Channel 4 comedy series that initially focused on the lives of the Gallagher family who lived on the fictional Chatsworth Estate, a deprived council estate in Manchester. A central character throughout all the eleven series that ran from 2004 to 2013 was unemployed, alcoholic and frequent drug user Frank Gallagher. The programme reflected then Prime Minister David Cameron's conception of a 'broken Britain'. *Shameless* addressed complex social and personal issues and strained relationships by presenting the lives and choices of working-class people as both tragic and comedic in nature. The format has been used to create an American version, a Turkish version and a Russian version of the series. The characters in *Shameless* are presented as people who lack the neoliberal aspirational spirit of self-crafting and 'graft' as the qualities to bring about upward mobility and market success.

From the fictional working-class characters Wayne and Waynetta Slob in the popular 1990s BBC comedy series *Harry Enfield & Chums*, Catherine Tate's character of Lauren Cooper in the BBC's *The Catherine Tate Show*, to the Vicky Pollard character in *Little Britain*. Beverly

Skeggs argues that Vicky Pollard is identified as the chav mum *par excellence*, incoherent, 'loud, white, excessive, drunk, fat, vulgar, disgusting' she embodies all the moral obsessions historically associated with young white working-class mothers in one iconic comic body (Skeggs 2006: 965).

Precarity is central to the shameless lifestyle, or what Imogen Tyler (2015) describes as a biopolitics of disposability and the recreation of the poor as national abjects. Henry Giroux also argues that contemporary urban life is characterised by a biopolitics of disposability in which 'poor minorities of color and class, unable to contribute to the prevailing consumerist ethic, are vanishing into the sinkhole of poverty in desolate and abandoned enclaves of decaying cities [and] neighbourhoods' (Giroux 2007: 309). The urban poor are subject to degrading labels such as chav, pikey or 'white trash'. To identify a person as a 'chav' is not simply reactive but constitutive of social class.

The same 'shameless' lifestyle is also found in a number of reality television shows. In reality TV, as in television comedy, the poor are presented as a rough, sub-proletarian section of the working class often labelled as 'chavs'; an abject group of vulgar and tasteless tragi-comic individuals who have excluded themselves from decent society. Although some reality TV programming looks and sounds like a freakshow, the underpinning message of the most downmarket, vulgar and poor-taste reality television promoting a core set of neoliberal cultural ideals. All reality TV programmes rely on humiliation of the participants in some fashion that allows the audience to observe and enjoy the victim's shame and discomfort.

A long-running and well-liked reality television show is MTV's *Geordie Shore*. The programme was originally focused on eight housemates: Gaz, Charlotte, Jay, Holly, Greg, Sophie, Vicki and James, who lived in a *Big Brother*-style house and viewers were invited to follow their 'party lifestyle' of clubbing, binge-drinking and having sex, framed ongoing within what Helen Wood (2016) describes as a 'spectacularisation' of the working class. The housemates are presented as:

> ungovernable, abject, revolting subjects who operate without shame, the very opposite to the self-regulating, good, neoliberal citizen. In this light, the show clearly perpetuates cruel and

regional stereotypes of the white working class, fuelling the hate figure of the 'CHAV', which has become a key symbol of abjection and social exclusion in neoliberal Britain.

(Wood 2016: 3)

The hostility towards the 'shameless' lifestyle of the urban poor came to the surface in 2008 in the case of Shannon Matthews, a 9-year-old girl from a West Yorkshire council estate who was the victim in a fake kidnap plot planned by her mother Karen Matthews and her boyfriend's uncle Michael Donovan. After Shannon was found, press attention turned towards Karen Matthews and focused on her moral failings. She was reported to have had seven children by five different men and two of her children were registered as having fathers that were unknown. The Karen Matthews case was highlighted by then Prime Minister David Cameron as evidence of his 'broken Britain' thesis. In 2008, David Cameron said, in an article he wrote for the *Mail on Sunday* (Cameron 2008), that tackling the 'broken society' was at the top of his policy agenda and he went on to describe the Shannon Matthews case as a 'verdict on our broken society'. Cameron's focus was on the personal moral failings of the individuals in poverty, not on the wider social causes of inequality:

The details are damning. A fragmented family held together by drink, drugs and deception. An estate where decency fights a losing battle against degradation and despair. A community whose pillars are crime, unemployment and addiction [...] Children whose toys are dad's discarded drink bottles; whose role models are criminals, liars and layabouts; whose innocence is lost before their first milk tooth [...] What chance for these children? Raised without manners, morals or a decent education, they're caught up in the same destructive chain as their parents. It's a chain that links unemployment, family breakdown, debt, drugs and crime. Breaking that chain means recognising the scale of the problem and taking serious, long-term action.

In a similar fashion to Sarkozy, Cameron attempted to blame residents of council estates for their own plight without relating the events to his own neo-liberal policies and their impact on the wider socio-economic conditions in the urban environment. Cameron's position can be understood in Bourdieu's terms as the use of estrangement as symbolic violence for political ends. Cameron was encouraging people to adopt his emotionally phrased political attempt to build upon the negative tabloid representations of the inhabitants of social housing for the purpose of political propaganda, blaming the victims for their lack of moral qualities and their own exclusion and inequality. Cameron's position has much in common with Martha Nussbaum's (2004: 107) argument that ideas of social hygiene and disgust have been used throughout history 'as a powerful weapon in social efforts to exclude certain groups and persons'. This form of disgust is used to maintain the boundaries between self and 'contaminating others' (Ngai 2005: 338–339).

Conclusion

This chapter has attempted to construct a quasi-Bourdieusian conception of the stranger. Estrangement often comes about as the product of a divided habitus and is experienced as a form of hysteresis, the relative value of the capital held by an individual may be valued in another field but not in the field that they currently find themselves. Symbolic violence underpins classification, recognition and misrecognition leading to an understanding of difference and the arbitrary exclusion of people within a system of constructed objective relations. Bourdieu's understanding of the relationship between agency and structure is *antidualistic* in its approach. It attempts to move beyond what he saw as the false opposition between subjectivist and objectivist modes of social analysis. Bourdieu does not suggest that people are programmed or conditioned to act only determined by the structured patterns within society; alternatively Bourdieu does not suggest that individuals are completely free to behave as they wish. However, there is an intersection of culture, social exclusion and power. A theory of human agency is not in itself an explanation of how or why something in the social structure happens. Agents are guided in their behaviour and for Bourdieu that guidance is provided by practice. Bourdieu develops an approach to understanding the relationship between individual human agency and the social structure that draws upon his three central concepts of habitus, field and practice. Strangers are individuals who are on the wrong side of the boundaries of the social field they find themselves in. And estrangement is the classification and placing of the Other as a person onto the other side of the border; a person who should be elsewhere not in their current field. The argument presented is that Bourdieu's concepts of habitus, field and practice generate social and economic inequalities and exclusion, and establish a boundary between the people who are assumed to belong and those who do not, the strangers. The processes of estrangement are often viewed as a form of transgression. The stranger finds themselves outside of the field-specific doxa and practice. Transgression can be viewed as threatening, as to transgress presupposes agency and to be seen to transgress is to demonstrate knowledge of constraint and the ability to step outside of constraint; to draw upon resources from outside of the symbolic field to step beyond the 'border'. To step outside of the taken for granted categories that make experiences intelligible is a situation that people who do not transgress find unnerving or even intimidating.

References

Alexander, J. (1995). *Fin de siècle social theory: Relativism, reduction, and the problem of reason*. London: Verso.

BBC (2012) Nicolas Sarkozy says France has too many foreigners. BBC online, 12 March 2012. https://www.bbc.co.uk/news/world-europe-17280647

Bourdieu, P. (1977) *Outline of a theory of practice*. Cambridge: Cambridge University Press.

Bourdieu, P. (1986) *Distinction: A social critique of the judgement of taste*. London: Routledge.

Bourdieu, P. (1991) *Language and symbolic power* (J. B. Thompson, ed., trans. G. Raymond and M. Adamson). Cambridge: Polity Press.

Bourdieu, P. (1998) *The state nobility: Elite schools in the field of power*, trans. L. C. Clough. Cambridge: Polity.

Bourdieu, P. (1999) *The weight of the world: Social suffering in contemporary society*, trans. P. Parkhurst Ferguson. Cambridge: Polity.

Bourdieu, P. (2000) *Pascalian meditations*, trans. R. Nice. Stanford, CA: Stanford University Press.

Bourdieu, P. (2001) *Masculine domination*. Cambridge: Polity Press.

Bourdieu, P. (2008) *Sketch for a self-analysis*. Cambridge: Polity Press.

Bourdieu, P. (2011) *On television*. Cambridge: Polity Press.

Bourdieu, P. and Eagleton, T. (1995) Doxa and common life: An interview. In T. Eagleton, (ed.), *Mapping ideology* (pp. 265–277). London: Verso.

Bourdieu, P. and Passeron, J. C. (1977) Reproduction. In *Education, society and culture*, trans. R. Nice. London: Sage.

Bourdieu, P. and Wacquant, P. (1992) *An invitation to reflexive sociology*. Cambridge: Polity.

Butler, J.(2004). *Precarious life: the powers of mourning and violence*. London and New York:Verso.

Cameron, D. (2008) There are 5 million people on benefits in Britain. How do we stop them turning into Karen Matthews? David Cameron for MailOnline8 December 2008. https://www.dailymail.co.uk/news/a rticle-1092588/DAVID-CAMERON-There-5-million-people-benefits-Britain-How-stop-turning-this.html

Fligstein, N. and McAdam, D. (2012) *A theory of fields*. Oxford: Oxford University Press.

Giroux, H. (2007) Violence, Katrina, and the biopolitics of disposability. *Theory Culture Society*, 24(7–8), 305–309.

Goffman, E. (1963) *Behaviour in public places*. New York: The Free Press.

Goffman, E. (1963a) *Stigma: Notes on the management of a spoilt identity*. Englewood Cliffs, NJ: Prentice-Hall.

Jobard, F. (2014) Riots in France: Political, proto-political, or anti-political turmoils? In D. Pritchard and F. Pakes (Eds), *Riot, unrest and protest on the global stage*. London: Palgrave Macmillan. ebook: 9781137305510.

Kafka, F.(2009/1915) *Metamorphosis*. Eastford:Martino Fine Books.

Kitagawa, E. M. and Taeuber, K. E. (1985) *The Chicago Community fact book*. Chicago Community Inventory. Chicago: University of Chicago Press.

Macé, E. (2005) Banlieues: des territoires abandonnés? *Le Monde* (November 7).

Ngai, P.(2005). *Made in China: Women factory workers in a global workplace*. Durham, NC:Duke University Press.

Nussbaum, M.(2004). *Hiding from humanity: Disgust, shame, and the law*. Princeton, NJ:Princeton University Press.

Samuel, H. (2007) Sarkozy blames Paris riots on 'thugocracy'. The *Telegraph* online, 29 November 2007. https://www.telegraph.co.uk/news/world news/1570927/Sarkozy-blames-Paris-riots-on-thugocracy.html

Skeggs, B.(2006)The making of class and gender through visualising moral subject formation. *Sociology*, 39(5), 965–982.

Tetreault, C. (2008) La racaille: Figuring gender, generation, and stigmatized space in a French cité. *Gender and Language*, 2(2), 141–170.

Turner, V. (1967) *The forest of symbols: Aspects of Ndembu ritual*. Ithaca, NY: Cornell University Press.

Turner, V. (1969) *The ritual process: Structure and anti-structure*. Piscataway, NJ: Aldine Transaction.

Tyler, I. (2015) Classificatory struggles: Class, culture and inequality in neo-liberal times. *The Sociological Review*, 63(2), 493–511.

Tyler, I. and Bennett, B. (2010) 'Celebrity chav': Fame, femininity and social class. *European Journal of Cultural Studies*, 13(3), 375–393.

Wacquant, L. (1996) The rise of advanced marginality: Notes on its nature and implications. *Acta Sociologica*, 39, 121–139.

Wacquant, L. (1998) Inside the zone: The social art of the hustler in the Black American ghetto. *Theory, Culture, Society*, 15(2), 1–36.

Wacquant, L. (1998a) Pierre Bourdieu. In R. Stones (ed.), *Key sociological thinkers* (pp. 215–229). Houndmills, Basingstoke: Macmillan.

Wacquant, L. (2001) Elias dans le ghetto noir. *Politix*, 56(4), 209–217.

Wacquant, L. (2004). Decivilizing and demonizing: The remaking of the black America ghetto. In S. Loyal and S. Quilley (Eds), *The sociology of Norbert Elias* (pp. 95–121). Cambridge: Cambridge University Press.

Wacquant, L. (2007) Territorial stigmatization in the age of advanced marginality. *Thesis Eleven*, 91, 66–77.

Wacquant, L. (2009) *Punishing the poor: The neo-liberal government of social insecurity*. Durham and London: Duke University Press.

Wacquant, L. (2012) Three steps to a historical anthropology of actually existing neoliberalism. *Social Anthropology*, 20(1), 66–79.

Wacquant, L. (2013) Symbolic power and group-making: On Pierre Bourdieu's reframing of class. *Journal of Classical Sociology*, 13(2), 274–291.

Wood, H. (2016) The politics of hyperbole on Geordie Shore: Class, gender, youth and excess. *European Journal of Cultural Studies*, 20(1), 39–55.

CONCLUSION

The stranger in contemporary society

The principal authors discussed in this book, Georg Simmel, Erving Goffman, Pierre Bourdieu, Norbert Elias and Zygmunt Bauman, were focused on attempting to explain stability in social life, and the processes of sociability, together with an understanding of how and why people choose to cooperate with one another within a social order. These issues remain continuing concerns for social science. In addition, all of these authors assume that humans are in general inclusive. However, the mechanisms that bring about a sense of community are the same mechanisms that generate estrangement. As such, not all people are included. In addition, some people are subjected to collective strategic actions that aim to change the constructed social order in such a way as to actively bring about their exclusion from social life. The process of barrier or border construction is the starting point for the processes of estrangement for all the principal authors examined in this book. The excluded individuals are the strangers. Zygmunt Bauman (2010) describes how, in *The Elementary Structures of Kinship* (1949), Claude Lévi-Strauss explained that the invention of incest, the identification of certain categories of individuals with whom it was acceptable to have sexual intercourse with and those with whom it was not, provided the first boundary for acceptable and unacceptable behaviour:

> Artificial divisions and distinctions imagined and imposed by
> humans were forced upon natural similarities and differences; more
> precisely, certain natural traits were injected with added meaning,
> through associating them with peculiar rules of perception, eva-
> luation and the choice of behavioural pattern.
>
> *(Bauman 2010: 167)*

All human beings have a common element because they are recognised
as 'people'. In addition, human beings also have self-definition/self-
identity and an ascribed or social identity. The person is never identified or defined by their humanity alone. Strangers are 'people' because
we can recognise them bodily, organically, physically etc. as human,
but our identity needs to be built upon factors that are in addition to
our humanity; people make a distinction between *what we are* as a
human being and *who we are*, human beings like us. It is the absence of
the additional element which 'we' feel we share but which the stranger
may not share that makes us question if the stranger is fully human. The
stranger may not be human enough to be regarded as 'one of us'.
Identification has both a personal or intimate element and an ascribed
or externally defined element. The balance between the personal/inti-
mate element and the ascribed/externally defined element has a central
role to play in the formation of our perceived identity and impacts on
our subjectivity. Boundaries set the limits of ordinary experience. The
position of the stranger within the group is fixed within a symbolic set
of human relations that are like spatial boundaries found in geographical
places. The stranger is an 'assembled being' and as such the stranger is
not a role but a configuration of the Other in our 'bordered imagination'. The notion of practice allows us to see that individual people are
the carriers and creators of borders and boundaries. We go through life
defining and redefining self and Other in relation to the guidance of
social practices, placing on one side or the other of a border that we
ourselves have contributed to the construction of.

A practice-based conception of the stranger views the process of
estrangement as something which is constructed within the everyday
activities of people like us, our habits and ordinary ways of behaving.
At the same time, once constructed, practice is a resource used for the
navigation of self. The relationship between agency and structure, or

the internal subject work of self and the external objective world of structure, is then never a simple picture. The relation between human beings and the real external world involves drawing upon the practices found in the external world but created by people to guide our subjectivity in such a way that we are comfortable with a socially approved subjectivity. We draw upon practice to define and shape self in relation to Others and to place oneself within the 'we' relationship, as an ordinary person within the group of similar ordinary people. Practice is a resource that we draw upon effectively to demonstrate to people around us that this is me and I belong.

Strangers are not very good at 'doing ordinary'. Estrangement is the perception of difference as a potential or real threat and the stranger is seen as the carrier of the threat to the individual self and the wider society. The stranger is 'not one of us', and although human agents are generally inclusive, they often find difference unnerving. A central aspect of inclusion is the need to keep difference to a minimum and to do this people feel secure when they engage in effective border creating and border maintaining. The processes of estrangement in contemporary society is then a creation of a changeable configuration of practices. People within the border are regarded as 'we', the ordinary people who are just like us and for that reason whom we feel the need to include. However, effective inclusion needs the Other who is different, who is not like us, not part of 'we' and who is strange. The stranger is the Other on the other side of the of the border that we have created. The stranger at the door can be unnerving because the presence of the stranger reminds us that there are other ways of leading a life. Such boundaries for acceptable behaviour are created to guide people on how to behave and to identify differences between acceptable and unacceptable behaviours in other people. Practices help to shape even the subtlest of our acts. The practices also constitute the boundaries we create and are understood as part of us; we live with them and through them. The boundary allows 'us' to identify between categories of people who behave in an acceptable or unacceptable way. In other words, between those who belong (us, the insiders) and those who do not (them), the strangers. Strangers are assumed to have a greater propensity to behave in an unacceptable way. Borders encourage us to think of difference as danger.

Although not all the principal authors looked at in this book directly address the issue of the stranger, they are all concerned with the process of Othering that underpins the processes of estrangement. By abstracting key points on the mechanisms of exclusion from the principal authors in our text, it is possible to say that the practices of estrangement operate at three interconnected levels of abstraction: the intrapersonal level, the inter-personal level and the structural level.

- At the intra-personal level: individuals have a fear and loathing of strangeness as a form of contamination, and out of anxiety search for it within themselves in order to expel it.
- At the inter-personal level: individuals have a fear and loathing of strangeness as a form of contamination and search for it within others in close proximity in order to avoid contagion.
- At the structural level: individuals have a fear and loathing of contamination as an external, societal threat.

Strangers are subjected to constraint and these constructed constraints are used to challenge the legitimacy of the stranger to be with 'us' inside the boundary. The process of barrier or border construction allows both social inclusion and exclusion to take place by the creation of a category of person as Other; a category of person as an outsider whom we should choose not to include. 'We' are predisposed to attempt to form a connection with people with whom we share a background but at the same time people are boundary creating and boundary maintaining. Inclusion is then maintained by the creation and imposition of a barrier or a border that is constructed out of habit, practice or some related form of human interaction that is part of a process of social construction of difference.

The barrier or border is used to identify a separation between those individuals whom 'we', on this side of the border, assume are like 'us' and are understood to be part of 'we'. On the other side of the border are 'they', the people whom 'we' assume are not like 'us'; they are the strangers. The border can take a physical form that is used to define a physical space in which only 'we' have a legitimate reason to inhabit. Alternatively, the border can be a metaphysical barrier to identify those people who although within our physical proximity are not one of 'us', not part of 'we'. The processes of estrangement are often viewed as a form of control over transgression. Transgression can be viewed as threatening, as the ability to transgress presupposes agency and to be seen to transgress is to demonstrate knowledge of constraint and the ability to step outside of constraint, to draw upon resources from outside of the symbolic field or to step beyond the 'border'. The stranger's assumed ability to step outside of the taken for granted categories that make experiences intelligible is a situation that people who do not transgress find unnerving or even intimidating, as the presence of the stranger makes our borders insecure.

The stranger is then an individual who may not be known to us personally, but that is not to say that the stranger is completely unknown. We may not know the individual, but we do know about people who are in the category that the stranger is part of. The placing of an individual within the meaningful category of stranger involves the imposition of meaning onto the unique individual, which diminishes what is unique about them to the degree that the individual becomes part of 'they': the person like all the other categories of person from the other side of the border; people who are known to us but not like us. Estrangement is then constructed around issues of potential transgression or contamination of the Other who has to be separated from 'us'. The potential transgression or contamination of the Other makes it uncomfortable for many of 'us' to engage with 'them'.

Reference

Bauman, Z. (2010) *44 letters from the liquid modern world*. Cambridge: Polity.

INDEX